MW01089128

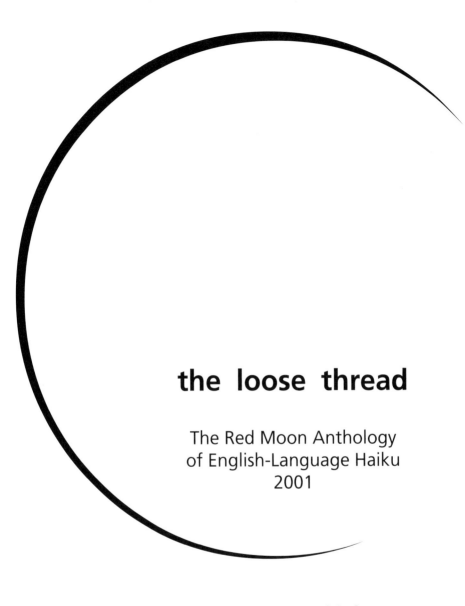

the loose thread

The Red Moon Anthology
of English-Language Haiku
2001

Jim Kacian ✧ **Editor-in-Chief**

Dimitar Anakiev ✧ **Jan Bostok**
Tom Clausen ✧ **Ellen Compton** ✧ **Dee Evetts**
Maureen Gorman ✧ **A. C. Missias**
Kohjin Sakamoto ✧ **Alan Summers** ✧ **George Swede**

Published by
Red Moon Press
P. O. Box 2461
Winchester VA
22604-1661 USA
redmoon@shentel.net

ISBN 1-893959-26-0

All work published in
the loose thread:
The Red Moon Anthology of
English-Language Haiku 2001
by permission of the individual authors
or their accredited agents.

Cover painting: *Blue III*
Joan Miró, 1961: oil on canvas.
Paris, Musée National d'Art Moderne,
Centre Georges Pompidou.
Used with permission.

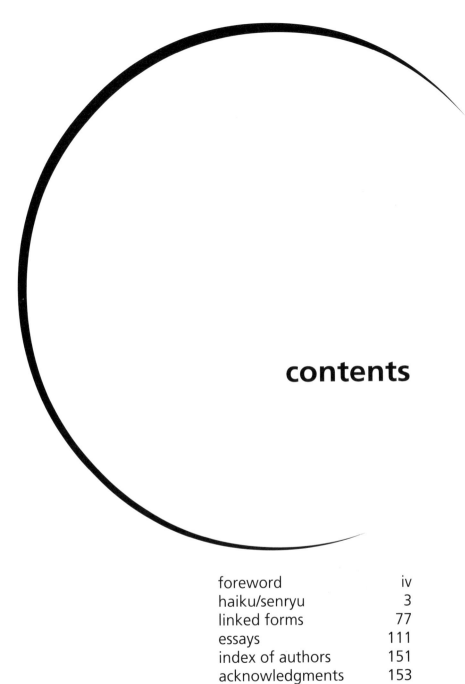

contents

foreword

HAIKU HAVE BEEN USED FOR ANY NUMBER OF PURPOSES. As PEN/Faulkner award-winning translator Hiroaki Sato avers in his *One Hundred Frogs*: "Hokku and haiku have been written to congratulate, to praise, to describe, to express gratitude, wit, cleverness, disappointment, resentment, or what have you, but rarely to convey enlightenment." Of course, in light of the haiku practice of the past 50 years, we cannot eliminate this usage, either. But we understand what Sato intends: to limit our understanding of what haiku may be to a kind of zen revelation is to reduce its variety, its scope, and most of all, its art.

It is clear that both traditions—haiku as art, haiku as zen expression—are flourishing, and there is no reason to insist that only the one or the other is "true". Haiku, if it is a serious art form, is capacious enough to contain both, and more. In fact, without this capacity, it would not be worthy of our full artistic study—its own limitations would diminish its importance.

At one point in the west's understanding of what haiku might be, some subject matter—poems of war, for example—would have been eschewed. But art must be capable of giving expression to the totality of our reality, all of our emotion and understanding. To rule important topics "out of bounds" would be the death-knell of haiku as serious art.

Of course, this has not been the case, as is evidenced in this volume and elsewhere. Haiku is capable of expressing all of the critical issues which face us as human beings today, and in the particular fashion which makes it unique. *The Red Moon Anthologies* aim to recognize the best of haiku regardless of the school out of which it arises, based on its relevance, yes, but most especially, based on its achievement as art. This is its most important legacy, and the only real argument why such work deserves to be retained in our literary heritage.

Jim Kacian
Editor-in-Chief

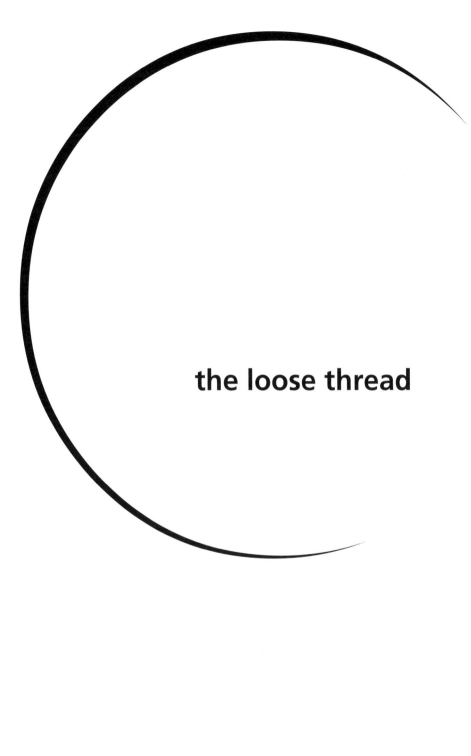

the loose thread

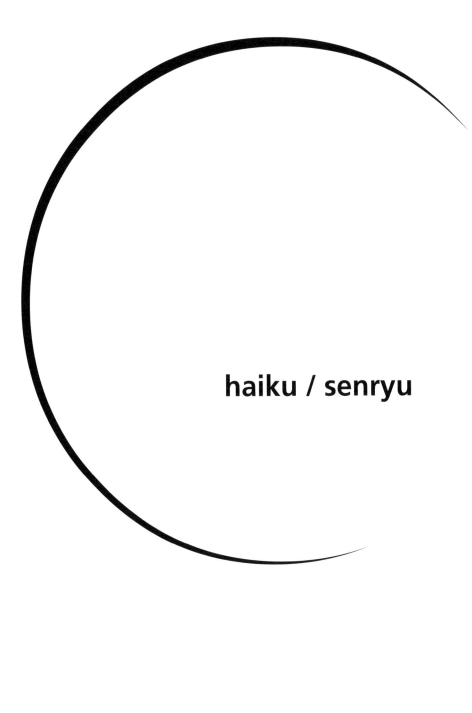

haiku / senryu

Stephen Addiss ✧ United States

late autumn—
love
without desire

ai li ✧ England

talk of divorce
she feels the knife edge
of her skirt's pleat

5

Bin Akio ✧ Japan

The snow on a cedar mountain
is elastic—
the first light of the New Year

odd g. aksnes ✧ Norway

empty corner
slowly the moon leaves
the dust

Francis Alexander ✧ United States

abandoned house—
the fallen branch stretches
the telephone wire

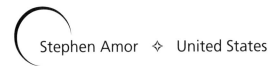

Stephen Amor ✧ United States

A moonlit night;
the firefly reappears
in a different spot.

 an'ya ✧ United States

After its first flight
the young gerfalcon's talons
tighter on my glove.

 Fay Aoyagi ✧ United States

Independence Day—
I let him touch
a little bit of me

Winona Baker ✧ Canada

breast self-examination
a moth batters
the screened window

Geri Barton ✧ United States

moving day
again, I pack the china
we never use

Gretchen Graft Batz ✦ United States

April sunrise
the soft call and response
of two barred owls

Cathy Drinkwater Better ✦ United States

heading into the sunset
the sister I don't talk to
one year older today

Gregg Billingsley ✧ England

suddenly
in a garden centre
becoming 30

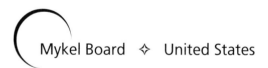

Mykel Board ✧ United States

fiftieth birthday
standing a little closer
to the toilet

Susan Bond ✧ Canada

> canyon
> hearing the loose stone
> again

Miriam Borne ✧ United States

> in the casket room
> the funeral director's children
> play hide and seek

Mark Brooks ✧ United States

new hammock—
my beer on the other side
of the porch

crescent moon
the gas pump handle
steals my warmth

withering wind
the fence-builder pulls a nail
from his lips

Randy Brooks ✧ United States

moonrise . . .
cattle single file through
the narrow pasture gate

early morning cool
men in hard hats gather
on the last patch of grass

Greeba Brydges-Jones ✧ New Zealand

arm in plaster
the weight
of a careless moment

Jonathan Buckley ✧ England

the ebb and flow
of sea between my legs
a passing girl

Yu Chang ✧ United States

old passport
the tug
of my father's smile

back at camp
the mountain peak
still in my legs

Tom Clausen ✧ United States

in her sleep
she steals back
her hand

David Cobb ✧ England

the trees move
only at their tips:
midsummer dusk

Kathy Lippard Cobb ✧ United States

scraping frost
off the windshield—
no words between us

john crook ✦ England

mid-autumn
the fridge magnet
slides to the floor

Michael Cross ✧ United States

      dinner alone—
        orchid shadows
      on the opposite chair

Joyce Walker Currier ✧ United States

      at my father's grave—
      the weight
      of unspoken words

DeVar Dahl ✧ Canada

empty cabin
the beached canoe
fills with leaves

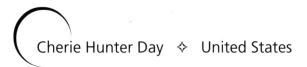

Cherie Hunter Day ✧ United States

cold snap—
the skittish crow sets off
an entire field

Andrew Detheridge ✧ England

on the country road—
turning off the headlights
to feel the darkness

Bruce Detrick ✦ United States

public garden
she photographs the blue iris
I just smelled

21

Steve Dolphy ✧ England

All Saints' Day
   closing the garage door
   on old shadows

Connie Donleycott ✧ United States

30th reunion—
raising our glasses
to see

Frank Dullaghan ✧ England

searching the cupboard
for the answer
to why I opened it

David Elliott ✧ United States

Hiking by full moon—
the rockslide a spill of light
down the mountain

Dee Evetts ✧ United States

store window
the young couple takes turns
testing the double bed

retuning
the guitarist turns to face
the subway wall

Michael Fessler ✧ Japan

closing time
bronze cupid
stops peeing

Stanford M. Forrester ✧ United States

winter afternoon—
a slow shadow fills
the empty bowl

25

Sandra Fuhringer ✧ Canada

changing light
the face of a woman
reading a letter

D. Claire Gallagher ✧ United States

a hairline crack
in the vase of daylilies—
water changing shape

Barry George ✧ United States

Making change—
the conductor shifts
his toothpick

Brian Gierat ✧ United States

approaching storm—
minnows dart
in the bait bucket

Ferris Gilli ✧ United States

divorce papers
she carefully snips
a loose thread

autumn wind
a small red dragon
warm from the kiln

chris gordon ✧ United States

drinking tea i didn't stop the war i just forgot about it

Maureen Gorman ✧ United States

silent car ride
after the argument
I adjust the heat

LeRoy Gorman ✧ Canada

exam silence
chalkdust settles
in the sun

the quiet graveyard
a warm breeze & an end
to alphabetic order

Caroline Gourlay ✧ Wales

below the door
of the photo booth
unlaced shoes

David Gross ✧ United States

snowed in
the old hen
too tough to eat

Carolyn Hall ✧ United States

January 3ʳᵈ
the Weight Watchers meeting
doubles in size

indian summer
both gardening gloves
worn through

Yvonne Hardenbrook ✧ United States

end of winter
a spot of sunlight inside
the potting shed

Jackie Hardy ✧ England

straight road ahead:
the shimmering mirage
keeps its distance

Kei Hayashi ✧ Japan

Breaking
my yellow crayon to draw
the barley harvest field

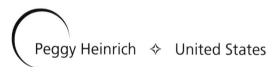

Peggy Heinrich ✧ United States

first contraction
stopping in the snowstorm
to buy cat food

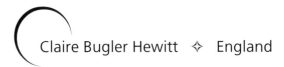

Claire Bugler Hewitt ✧ England

newly pregnant—
the light around my shadow
in the field

eric l. houck, jr. ✧ United States

separating fog
from fog
strand of barbed wire

Ken Jones ✧ Wales

Aging address book
the living squeezed
between the dead

Patrick Kelly ✧ United States

light snowfall
the tick of an engine
cooling

Jim Kacian ✧ United States

just now
as my life turns crazy
forsythia

the melon splits
ahead of my knife—
midsummer heat

sundown—
one dog starts
them all

Jerry Kilbride ✧ United States

day after diagnosis
avoiding my eyes
while shaving

Valeria Krestova ✧ Russia

guests gone . . .
I eat again
from the cracked plate

Robert Kusch ✧ United States

missed the train
—a small green shoot
between the tracks

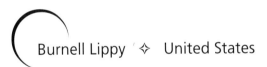

Burnell Lippy ✧ United States

a cricket
where the mortar's gone
September evening

Leatrice Lifshitz ✦ United States

alone—
she takes the daisies
from room to room

land's end—
sand in each bite
of my apple

Rebecca Lilly ✧ United States

A warm breeze . . .
the scent of hay bales
from the moonlit field

Cold autumn dusk—
fog mantles the bridge
where the suicide jumped

Matthew Louvière ✧ United States

first light
the old rooster crows
one white breath

Robert Mainone ✧ United States

all around
light failing in a field
of fireflies

paul m. ✧ United States

Indian summer
the trolley conductor
forgets to charge me

a coyote call
goes unanswered
evening star

Steve Mason ✧ England

> argument at dinner
> a fly moves
> from plate to plate

Paul David Mena ✧ United States

> snow mixes with rain—
> my mother keeps calling me
> by my brother's name

David Meyers ✧ Canada

church exit—
they pick up the argument
where they left it

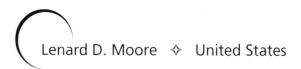

Lenard D. Moore ✧ United States

funeral procession
the stillness of cotton blossoms
in sunlight

A. C. Missias ✧ United States

reading the poems
of a lost friend—
summer rain

veterans' cemetery—
a wide expanse of lawn
beyond the graves

holding her hand;
the pattering
of summer rain

 Matt Morden ✧ Wales

shortlisting . . .
a hint of perfume
on the résumé

 Marlene Mountain ✧ United States

just enough rain to moisten the lips of the wild lily

Naia ✧ United States

heat wave—
the fly's iridescence
just before the swat

John Ower ✧ United States

lovers on the beach
the moon draws the ocean
to their toes

Pamela Miller Ness   ✧   United States

Alzheimer's ward
snow fills the sill
of his empty room

her dead mother's room
opening the window
to let out a moth

vacation over—
hearing the sea
in the traffic's roar

W. F. Owen ✧ United States

summer wind—
a dragonfly grips
the clothespin

prostate exam
the doctor and I
trade jabs

her estate
dividing
the children

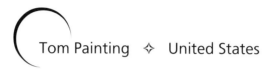

Tom Painting ✧ United States

family plot
the gravedigger
severs a root

solicitation
the wildlife activist
flashes her teeth

Christopher Patchel ✧ United States

bitter cold
a snowplow's scrape
in the night

midnight stars
our stroll through the neighborhood
trips light after light

spring fever—
pedaling my new bike
through the scents

Matthew Paul ✦ England

> my train delayed
>   by a suicide—
> Easter drizzle

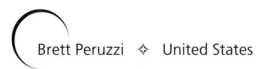

Brett Peruzzi ✦ United States

> deep summer—
> the sweet-smelling wake
> of a hay wagon

Joanna Preston   ✧   New Zealand

hospice visit   he still beats me at chess

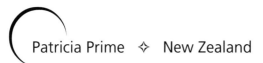

Patricia Prime   ✧   New Zealand

mending his fence
the neighbor's mouth
full of nails

Anthony J. Pupello ✧ United States

blustery wind
the dog walker sorts
a tangle of leashes

William Ramsey ✧ United States

afternoon light
on the sill
his urn's warmth

Linda Robeck ✧ United States

winter waves
she folds and unfolds
her layoff notice

back from the PO—
an empty space
where the manuscript was

Patricia Anne Rogers ✧ United States

birthday snow—
she erases her footprints
with a broom

Eric Rutter ✧ United States

in the next fitting room
a woman tells her husband
whether his pants fit

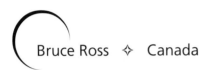

Bruce Ross ✦ Canada

early spring
the cemetery side gate
open a little

dense rain clouds
the small blue tent over
the open grave

morning fog
the ladder higher than
the house

Steve Sanfield   ✧   United States

$200 a night
but in the hotel fountain
only pennies

Robert Scotellaro   ✧   United States

as she talks of aging—
smoothing the creases
in her grocery bag

Rob Scott ✧ Netherlands

still no word
the moon
through another window

Semimaru ✧ Japan

A child of God—
will he be circumcised?
the spring Milky Way

R. A. Stefanac ✧ United States

communion wafer
she sticks out
her pierced tongue

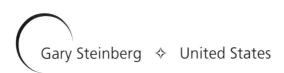

Gary Steinberg ✧ United States

winter rain I finger each seam on the baseball

John Stevenson ✧ United States

last piece
of a jigsaw puzzle...
filling in the sky

hazy moon
what to say
to your machine

tax return
pressing the air out of
the sealed envelope

Richard Stevenson ✧ Canada

memorial gun—
sticks, stones and candy wrappers
stuffed down the barrel

Susumu Takiguchi ✧ England

moonless night
I throw a beetle
into deep darkness

 Hilary Tann ✧ United States

eye exam
i stop trying
so hard

hotel room
watching the Weather Channel
for news of home

Rick Tarquinio ✧ United States

sent back out
for something I forgot
winter stars

Tom Tico ✧ United States

Thanksgiving:
having the flat
all to myself

Maurice Tasnier ✧ England

all her troubles
by my third pint I am
so understanding

recalling the days
it sounded like a flower
dementia . . .

Marc Thompson ✧ United States

a small white church
at the highway stoplight
evening rain

steady rain . . .
the man on the ladder
adjusts his cap

Cor van den Heuvel ✧ United States

a drop of water
floats by the canoe
on a curled leaf

the rusted paperclip
has stained my old poem
wind in the eaves

deep snow
the amusement park lit
by a single bulb

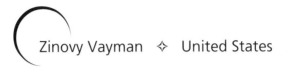

Zinovy Vayman ✧ United States

forest path:
when it becomes a fork
we turn back

David Walker ✧ England

wearing the suit
we shared
to your grave

Linda Jeannette Ward ✧ United States

heat waves—
the hitchhiker shifts her child
to the other hip

wind shift—
he plans a new route
for her wheelchair

Billy Watt ✧ Scotland

"Zen for Beginners",
with the remote control
lying on top.

Michael Dylan Welch ✧ United States

the silence between us
a quail finds its way
through the underbrush

Alison Williams ✧ England

darkness gathers
in the tree tops
crow by crow

Peter Williams ✧ England

five days later
counting the syllables
of my mother's illness

72

 Billie Wilson ✧ United States

an open book
on the old porch swing—
first fireflies

 Jeff Winke ✧ United States

Amtrak depot
a large man's yawn
connects two announcements

Ryuji Yamagishi ✧ Japan

On the chair
in the moonlight
different silences

Toshiro Yoshida ✧ Japan

Man will lean
someday, a ladder
against the Milky Way

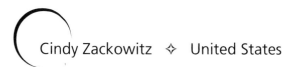

Cindy Zackowitz ✧ United States

unseasonable heat—
a woodpecker
in the lightning scar

Alenka Zorman ✧ Slovenia

dry laundry—
the fish pattern towel
still damp

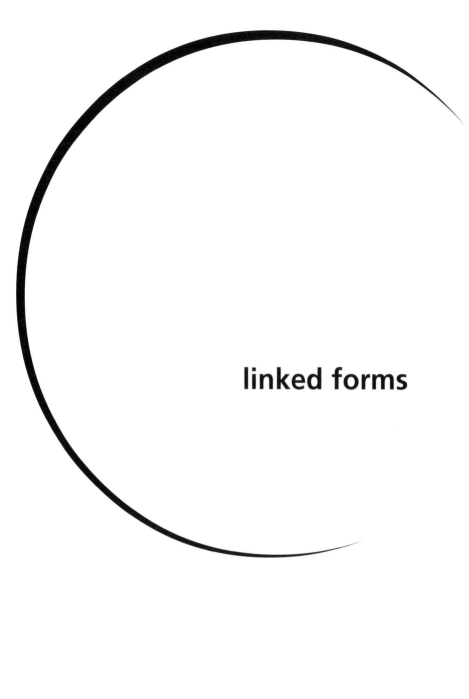

linked forms

Yu Chang ✧ United States

Refrigerator

ONE DAY LAST SUMMER, my old refrigerator suddenly quit. When the repairman handed me the culprit, a broken heating element, I happily paid $75 to get my refrigerator back. After that, it worked nicely except for hot days. Then, the motor would moan noticeably but there was no cooling at all. The thought of getting a new one did cross my mind, but I never got around to it.

The fridge's condition got worse in the middle of June this year. "That's it," I said to myself and headed for the mall. When I was removing the postcards and stickers to prepare the old fridge to be trucked away, a yellowed Christmas card caught my eye. The message inside read, "Merry Christmas! Hope everybody is fine. See you in New York. Love, Siv."

Siv Engstrom grew up in Göteberg, Sweden, but had spent many years abroad both in Europe and in the US by the time I met her. She was the happiest person I'd ever known, and she brought out the best in everyone. Siv particularly loved Britain, so much so that she bought a dilapidated English cottage near Cambridge. Restoration had already begun in the summer of 1988. Siv never made it to New York that year. She made it as far as Lockerbie, Scotland.

new fridge
the motor's faint hum
still there

79

David Cobb ✧ England

Down Epiphany Way

IN BERLIN ON A LATE SUMMER'S DAY the Epiphanienweg leads to a cemetery called Luisenfriedhof. I am coming to see you, Corporal Gabler. My second visit. After fifty years.

Monuments face each other across the gravel path, so that the acute morning sun, creating a pattern of serried shadows, strikes the blank rears of those on my left, while lighting up the inscribed faces of those on my right.

The place is full of flowers and German widows. The widows stare at me, they tend graves, some of them recording loved ones born in the very year you died in. Almost-old-comrade in the enemy's army, on the last day of the war you had a Russian bullet in the head, in the street outside your home, wearing your civvies. And me now, obligated to bring you the news of your widow, she too lying at peace, though in a corner of some English field.

Weren't we all three confirmed Romantics? The triangle has to be closed.

The sun is very warm today and, traversing row after row of tombstones, I can't find you anywhere. As I speak to you, *Wo steckst du denn?*, I wonder if it's in order to call you *du*. We were never properly introduced, we never even spoke. Just I stood beside her at the grave, holding a trowel that had lost its shape, while she laid flowers on you. That day, also in summer.

Rest, we all wished you rest, thinking of peace for

ever. *Ewige Ruh'*. But now, fifty years on, when I ask the gardener with a watering can in his hand where you might be concealed, he shakes his head, tells me—and I know he means help—to ask at the office. A plot for Gabler? Maybe his tenure . . . ?

> 'Rest in Peace'—
> and just nearby a plaque,
> 'Lease expired.'

I cannot face the office, go to the Lietzenseepark instead, where "the public are requested to respect the local residents' need of quietness." A Turkish family are spreading out a picnic, a Chinese woman goes through the unhurried postures of Tai-Chi, weeping willows touch the surface of the lake. It is still beautiful, do you remember the tulips, *Liebchen*? I think of sitting down in Babylon and weeping, and in that moment a faint shower begins.

> a sound I can't hear
> the consciousness of leaves
> receiving rain . . .

Ion Codrescu ✧ Romania

Towards a Mountain Temple

even through mist
the light finds its way . . .
old temple bell

EARLY MORNING. I open the window and look outside. Suddenly, I feel the moisture which comes into my room. I sip my jasmine tea and at the same time I look at the unfolded map. I take a last look before going towards the mountain temple. The English explanations are written under the Chinese text, which is smaller. To get to the narrow stepping path, I have to walk many hours on a forestry road which goes through two villages and one hamlet. I take my knapsack and say goodbye to the host where I stayed only one night.

parting time—
the host offers the guest
some dewy plums

The road ascends through bamboo, cedar, pine forests and other trees whose names I've forgotten. From time to time, a bird call crosses the mist. I can't see beyond thirty metres. All is gray and it's difficult to distinguish the outline of the trees, plants and rocks. Everything seems unreal. The landscape is like an ink painting where the strong strokes and details have disappeared. It's so quiet that I can hear the dewdrops falling on me from the branches of the tall pines.

82

lonely mountain road—
how smooth the surface
of the rock

After an hour of climbing, I pause beside a large stone covered with brushwood and I take a swig of the tea I have with me. I find it strange that I have not met anyone—neither travellers nor wood-cutters. Time passes while I am gazing at the dense forest, at the branches of the old trees that come together overhead and are so tangled. After some minutes a native approaches and stops his horses, and then invites me to take a seat in his cart. Guessing the place where I will go he pronounces loudly the name of the temple. In my turn, I confirm his intuition and say the same words. His face brightens up and his eyes look at the mountain peak. After some moments, by an interjection, he starts his horses. The sound of the cart and the clatter of hooves are all I hear in the silence of the mountain.

a broken tree—
it's apricot picking time
in my country

After we pass through the two villages the mist begins to rise. The landscape can be seen far away. Unnoticeably cedars and bamboos grow more and more rare. We approach the hamlet. From near the first house two children with their hands up run toward us. They shout the same words. When they notice that in the cart there is a foreigner, their voices fade and they become ashamed. My guide is their father. He stops the horses and raises the children onto the cart, one after another, even though their house is no more than twenty-five or thirty metres away. The faces of the children are radiant. Near their house, I get out from the cart and bend my head to thank my guide. Saying again the name of the temple he points out the place where the path begins through the woods towards the peak.

a gust of wind—
fern leaves cover and uncover
the small white mushroom

Even after the fog disappears, the moisture is on my clothes, plants and the air is full of resin scent. In the sunbeams the dewdrops sparkle. I watch the pine needles, which end with tiny, gleaming dewdrops. Butterflies zigzag around me and I wonder where they stayed hidden until now. Deep in the woods, sometimes loudly, sometimes gently, I hear a wood-cutter. Worn down by time and by the steps of countless pilgrims who came to visit the temple, the stone steps are slippery and I must pay attention to each. After half an hour of difficult climbing, I stop for a short while. From far away I can barely hear the waterfall. I continue to climb and the roaring of the water is louder and louder. Unexpectedly, on the narrow path a terrace and a pavilion appear in front of me. I enter the pavilion to sit on a bench and gaze towards the waterfall. Its water is completely white.

as I
approach
to watch
the waterfall
a lonely
bird
leaves
its place

The peaks alternate far away, one by one, like petrified ships floating above a still sea made of white clouds. Suddenly I remember the first Chinese reproductions I saw when I was a teenager. At that time I thought that Chinese mountains are only the fantasy of the painters and that their shapes are not real. Now I have the impression that the mountains I see are a copy of those paintings. I am thinking of Wang Wei, the poet-painter, who wrote in a poem:

> I notice a lonely far away peak
> which vanishes among clouds

As in Wang Wei's poem, this landscape I admire behind the waterfall, far away, a solitary summit is gradually covered, and disappears into the sea of clouds. Sometimes I think that only art copies nature. In this moment I realize that nature imitates art, too.

Near me, another peak, flooded by the light of the sun, is full of green due to the pine trees. In classic Chinese painting a green mountain means stability and a white cloud suggests instability, wandering. To know a mountain you must wander through its paths, woods and rocks, hearing its sounds and voices, watching it from far away or drawing it. Frederick Frank wrote that "Drawing is the discipline by which I constantly rediscover the world. I have learned that what I have not drawn I have never really seen, and that when I start drawing an ordinary thing I realize how extraordinary it is, sheer miracle: the branching of a tree, the structure of a dandelion's seed puff. I discover that among *The Ten Thousand Things* there is no ordinary thing. All that is, is worthy of being seen, of being drawn." I take the brush, the paper and the ink, and paint the landscape. Then I'll go towards the mountain temple.

> the last brush stroke—
> a dewdrop falls
> on my ink sketch

John J. Dunphy   ✧   United States

The Wall

THE POLISHED BLACK GRANITE of the Vietnam Veterans Memorial in Washington DC—popularly known as The Wall—subtly reflects its visitors. While reading the names of the over 58,000 Americans killed during that conflict, we suddenly realize that our images are transposed on those names.

This experience is especially poignant for 'Nam vets seeking the names of those with whom they served. They will never know a closer reunion with their fallen comrades.

> Vietnam Memorial
> aging veterans reflected on
> names of young men

David Elliott ✧ United States

Through the Silence

Another meal refused—
  "Is this what you want?"
my father slowly nods

      Late at night
        one goose flies through
          the silence

Dying? maybe
but out of the silence
he opens his eyes and winks

      Sorting Dad's old letters—
        across the street
        a leaf blower

The night of his death
  a few crickets
  and light rain

      His favorite chair—
      dent in the cushion
        not my size

  so small
  the bag of ashes
beside the newly dug hole

      After Dad's death
      so many Christmas cards
      wishing him well

Juan Escareal ✧ United States
Peggy Willis Lyles ✧ United States
Ferris Gilli ✧ United States

Talons in the Chimney

autumn wind
a styrofoam dish scrapes
the darkness

        chalk across the blackboard
        a shiver up my spine

softly tapping
on a bedroom window
the strangler fig

        soundless the clamp
        of a Venus flytrap

open flue
talons in the chimney
flush out soot

        stroke of midnight
        an owl screeches twice

Arwyn Evans ✧ Northern Ireland

Winder 1950

SATURDAY MORNING. I help my father count the takings at the Pithead Baths

Now for *that treat,* he says.

We cross the yard the tram rails to the East Pit winding house; enter its small door:

The smell steam and hot oil.

The sense of something breathing in its sleep.

The vast wheel drum I'm overawed.

We walk a little further following the warm handrail.

The gleam of polished steel fills the dim-lit hall

Gently the pistons start to move. The huge wheel slowly turns.

Gains speed.

Pistons feed-back valve-rods brass balled governors awhirl all in concert.

Though most of all the ponderous drive rod's thrust

> The lunge and swing
> of massive cams—
> their milk-smooth flow

Such momentum nothing, it seems, could make it cease.

But just as smoothly all slows down. Comes to soft rest.

> The sigh between
> my waking dreams

Vigil

An ant circles the "O" of October—Circus Maximus, carved in granite. A rain of hay drifts at the turning post. The sound of the mowers far above, blue sky of another world . . . The rest of the letters and numbers—your full name/your empty dates: the simple maze of 8, the oxbow of S, the great serpentine without its Versailles, the drained locks of H, its empty artificial waterways. The great moulds emptied of molten summer. The prison yards, pristine canals, the stalls and slave quarters of E.

> laying above you
> tracing the Braille
> of your name

The boys on riding mowers, their fluttering open legged khakis, legs with their dark growth of hair, close cropped summer haircuts consciously ungainly, spoiling to mar the beauty *you* will see to, dead or alive. All the things you would say like a hive at the end of summer.

> teenage mower
> rests his gas can
> on someone's grave

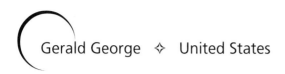

Gerald George ✧ United States

Arizona

Though a visitor, I could see how this place would drive any sensitive person to ecological radicalism. Flagstaff sprawls right under extraordinarily beautiful, emotionally powerful mountains. So life there, if you really are alive, is engagement with them, and becomes a fight to protect what makes you want to live from the landscape's death through commercial indifference. "Nature" itself rebels.

> spreading all over
> the deserted parking lot
> sweet smelling pine cones

A pumice mine's cancerous encroachment on a national forest preserve has in fact provoked a protest, which, shedding years of professional caution, I joined. After all, some company is gouging the mountain so that thirteen-year-old counter-fashion fashionables can dress themselves in "stone-ground" jeans! The voracious bulldozers were gouging way down in the bottom of the life-stripped canyon they are savagely widening, but we got the "media" out to see and kept the pressure on.

> saving the planet
> me and ten kids in a
> rusty truck

Afterwards, we went to the mountains' other side

91

to see ancient structures left by people who could build beautifully but lacked the technical sophistication to devastate the landscape: rock-mason predecessors of the Hopi.

> alone, a stone ruin
> white clouds pile
> silently

Through the afternoon, while the bright sun gave brilliance to the Painted Desert miles off in one direction, dark clouds accumulated over the peaks above Flagstaff in the other. How the hard-scrabble prehistoric dwellers must have looked back and forth each way, struggling to conceive a theology of adequate power and glory, especially when the sky grew wild over the fifteen visible, black peaks and lightning erupted.

> rumble of thunder
> quick gust of chill breeze
> a lizard skitters

Nonetheless, we stopped at another site, and almost reached an "overlook" before the long-building rainstorm struck. Even to me it seemed sacrilege to unfurl an umbrella, though the wind grew frighteningly fierce, scaring us back down to the safety of the one building at the site's entrance.

> hiding
> in the park latrine
> rain roof-battering

Later, the storm long gone, we found the little house, where I was to spend the night, via dirt roads through over-grazed scrub-land (how quickly one

can learn to regret cattle!), on which, notwithstand-
ing, delightful junipers and pinyon pines survive,
and astonishing cactus clusters. Lonely, desolate—
but there, such words described attractions.

> over the dark rim
> the setting sun burns down:
> a juniper fire

> desert night sounds
> I try to hear as if
> I weren't here

Carolyn Hall ✧ United States

Protective Coloration

ON THE STREET WHERE I GO FOR TAKE-OUT BURRITOS you can also buy old Wedgewood stoves and Westing-house fridges, new and used books, old and new clothing, low-fat lattés, and assorted recreational drugs. It's what my mother used to call a colorful neighborhood. It was there that I went to pick up the main course for a casual dinner with friends.

> underside
> of the red canvas awning
> not faded

Heading back to my car with beers, soft drinks, and burritos and chips for a party of six, browsing at sidewalk sales was clearly not on my agenda. But there, just in my path, a homeless man was empty-ing the contents of his grocery cart onto the pave-ment, hoping to sell what he could. At first glance, I thought there was nothing here to waylay me. But next thing I knew, I had set my bags on the ground and was sorting through his meager belongings. Just under a pile of wrinkled shirts, I found them— two trays of colorful butterflies pressed under glass. "How much?" I said—then paid him what he asked.

Later, after our dinner guests had gone, I inspected my purchases to see just what I had bought. They were scientific specimens illustrating the principle of mimicry. According to legends printed on the back, in each tray a butterfly distasteful or poisonous to birds was displayed beside an innocuous butterfly which looked so much like its noxious cousin that it was shunned by predators.

in the appliance store doorway
calling a Maytag box
home

Next time I went to the burrito shop, I looked for that man to ask how he came to possess these wonderful things. There were several men with grocery carts—but I couldn't recognize whether the man who'd sold me the butterflies was among them.

city lights
trying to make out
the constellations

Ken Jones ✧ Wales

Autumn Gothick

THE NIGHT STORM HOWLS round the gables, rattles the casements, growls down the chimney, and lashes the windows. Hour by hour we toss and turn.

Only half awake, I venture out into the dawn light. The wind chimes have been silenced and hanged high on an oak. Beside the cottage, Nant Sebon the Soapy Brook is foaming off to join the Rheidol as fast as it can go. And the patio presents a shocking sight.

> Plastic chairs tossed
> where they fell—
> a nasty incident

Only the table remains unmoved

> On the picnic table's marble top
> all winter long
> this smooth round stone

The pond has a ruffled clarity. The stream which feeds it comes roaring out of Coed Simdhe Llwyd— Grey Chimney Wood—at one end, and cascades over the drystone dam at the other. In the middle:

> Beneath the troubled surface
> a moaning hoard
> of well-washed acorns

The water laps the lotus throne of the walnut wood
Buddha and the claws of the pewter Pictish war-dog.

> World Honoured One
> a lapful
> of dead leaves

The war-dog has his ears back.

From the pond a flight of steps rises through dripping
ferns.

> Tops of the steps a watchman
> tall scrap iron stanchion
> his face a rusty bolt

Up here is a place of moss and many stones. Some
have attitude, while others are quite humble.

> Comes the rain
> and every small half-buried stone
> reflects the light

Jim Kacian ✧ United States

Three Short Haibun

EVERY THANKSGIVING I HEAD NORTH to visit my mother in the town I grew up in. Like the town, she's thin and failing. This will be the last time.

> half-way home
> I miss my turn—
> the century oak now gone

•

a long trip is promised, and this just the beginning, and i don't know where it is exactly i am to go or how i am to get there, just that the going is what matters, and i have agreed to go, and am going

> into my dream
> the gentle rocking
> of the ship

•

in the heart of the hubbub "peace officers" from sweden switzerland holland & united states walking the mid-day heat stopping here to cool on leave from the action in kosovo i too cooling after a hike across the bridge to the old albanian side of town a bazaar with rugs and metals and spitted chickens but no luck on the coffee grinder i covet then up to the fortress overlooking the vardar where d and i compare notes on the cosmopolitan life of skopje which is the best Balkan solution to date cosmopolitan multicultural hospitable but doomed in the near future by internal rumblings of nationalism here the smoke of many rises commingles beneath the canopy and up alongside the building past a poster for the eponymous fyfo who aspires to be mayor the smoke haze dims him ever so slightly & seems to make him wave . . .

Dusanow bridge—
a stranger stops to light
my cigarette

Michael Ketchek ✧ United States

Lunar Eclipse

MY FRIEND FRANK AND I are driving through a snow-storm on the way to Bare Hill in hope of seeing the total eclipse of the moon. The radio warns us there is a travel advisory, and all unnecessary travel is discouraged. We laugh a bit foolishly at this advice coming over the airwaves.

snowstorm—
out on this eclipse night
only lunatics

Bare Hill, a place revered by the Seneca Indians, rises from the shore of Canandaigua Lake into a large broad hill that overlooks the lake and the surrounding country. The sacredness of the hill, the chance that the storm front will move through, along with more than our fair share of dumb luck are what Frank and I are counting on in our quest to see the eclipse.

driving by faith . . .
from the farmer's windblown field
blinding snow

Because of the storm we are running late and are ten minutes from Bare Hill at the time the eclipse is beginning, but it is still snowing so we don't feel as if we are missing anything. We notice that the snow is no longer falling heavily and we take this as an omen that it might clear altogether later that night and some of the eclipse will be visible to us. Suddenly Frank who is driving points at the windshield. "Look."

A glowing orb
mysterious behind clouds
missing a sliver

Both of us are stunned to see the eclipse through the now gently falling snow. After an hour and a half of tense driving we slap each other five and exult in our good fortune. A few minutes later we are driving up the side road that leads to the Bare Hill parking area, pleased that it is plowed all the way to the top, something that does not happen every winter. We jump out of the car into bitter cold. Clouds rush past, covering then uncovering, stringing whispy trails swiftly across the eclipsing moon.

the wild wind
carries our howls
to the moon

Even though it is cold (checking a wind-chill chart the next day I estimate that it felt like thirty below) we are exuberant. Frank has taken a drum from his car and is beating a primal rhythm. Wearing a parka and hiking boots I am dancing in the snow-reflected moonlight that waxes and wanes according to the wind-driven clouds.

Then it happens the last bit of silver crescent is gone and magically moments later the sky clears completely. Orion the Hunter and hundreds of other stars shine brightly in the clear winter sky. The moon glows dimly orange like a pumpkin, or rather like a lit but uncarved jack-o-lantern.

In the car there is a thermos of hot ginger tea and a bottle of scotch. We pour ourselves a cup of tea and pass the bottle back and forth several times. Then we walk a couple hundred yards to the edge of the nature preserve where a mutual friend has a tiny cabin.

> the wood so cold
> in the cast iron stove
> before it's lit

Forty minutes later we are barely getting warm when we leave the shelter of the cabin for the blustery wildness of Bare Hill and the rebirth of the moon. That is not how we think of it as we walk out into the cold, but it is how we will think of it in a few minutes, and any time after that. We stand in the biting wind gazing at the orange ball in the sky. The lower left edge is getting lighter. It even seems to bulge a little.

> bursting out
> of itself, a silver
> speck of moon

Frank and I are both awed by the sight. It is wondrous in an indecipherable way. All the science of converging orbits and celestial shadows is lost in the moment. There is just this outpouring of joy at the reappearance of some of the moon in its bright form.

> glowing silver
> starts to creep across
> the orange disk

It is powerfully cold and we start walking to keep warm. We finally stop when we come to a stand of pines that offers shelter from the wind. We find a spot where the pines are spaced a bit farther apart and through a gap in the branches view the moon as it slowly becomes full once more. Then we hurry back to the cabin cold, but feeling as if we have been blessed by being able to witness this extraordinary event. We feel fulfilled in ways we don't understand, nor do we try to, happy just to somehow have been part of this cosmic occasion.

> warming my feet
> by the stove, glancing
> again out the window

Michelle V. Lohnes ✧ Canada
Marco Fraticelli ✧ Canada

Two Swans: A Septenga

rubble lining the pond
two swans
share soggy bread

> *the taste of coffee*
> *in her kiss*

tossed kitchen scraps
the compost pile growing
black eyed susans

> *geese*
> *gathering dried weeds*

off to work
colours of autumn
stuck on the windshield

that red tree
outside the tennis court

late November
and still white blossoms
in the flower box

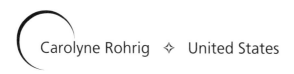

Carolyne Rohrig ✧ United States

Visit to the Mall

THE AIR IS CRISP this spring at the mall. The stores are not open yet. The French bakery is the only place doing business this early. With *café au lait* and *baguette* I sit outdoors in the early morning sun.

I'm waiting to see a friend of many years. This is her favorite mall and she visits it almost daily. She's schizophrenic. Her illness makes her refuse all medical help and intervention is against the law in California, so she remains untreated. I wait several hours. Just when I am about to give up, she suddenly appears. I notice dark circles under her eyes and her blouse and pants are dirty, but neat. The people around us stare. She recognizes me. She stops a few yards from my table. "Hello, Are you visiting?" she asks. "Yes, I came to see you. Can I buy you a cup of coffee?" "Sure," she smiles. "I'll be right back." She walks on and is swallowed up by the crowd of shoppers.

looking over my shoulder—
my seat already taken
by another woman

105

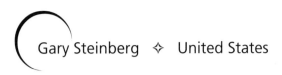

Gary Steinberg ✧ United States

Haibun

I DRAW BACK THE SHADES to reveal the mountain across the valley. The peak just begins to show a trace of redness. The sky to the west still contains stars dotting the fading blackness. I drain the remaining drops from a cup of green tea, and place it carefully on the window ledge.

> daybreak
> all at once the absence
> of stars

Turning from the window I take two steps towards my cushion. With the first step comes excitement and with the second fear and the narrative question: "Why exactly do I do this?" I sit for morning practice. Same time, same place, same practice. Yet somehow, like the sky, it is different every morning. I set the timer for an hour, draw my legs into their best facsimile of a half-lotus and straighten my back. Too straight as usual, overcompensating for poor posture. Pressing the start button I sigh as my eyes shut to the darkness of the room. I know that I'm in for a show this morning.

> sunrise
> as the bell fades
> thought resonates

In the darkness, investigating the facets that make

up my self-concept: possessions, job, social status, friends, children and relationships. This body, these emotions, and the thoughts that flit in and out of awareness. All that we take ourselves to be are dependent upon conditions. By their very nature these conditions are everchanging and so intertwined that they are unfathomable. I walk the razor's edge between contemplation and unrestrained thought as mind is again and again drawn towards the crescendo of this practice.

spring morning—
the curve of her back
in a distant bed

What will be? Of all the mind and body pheno-mena rising into the moment, this thought bullies itself to the forefront. Again and again I relax against it only to find mind suddenly and aggressively attack it. A vicious dog choking itself on the stout chain that fetters it. To confuse me, it changes forms. How-when-why? Swiftly and precisely it becomes why not? Different outfits on the same mannequin. Suddenly, it becomes obvious that there is no answer, except the one that rings of a yielding and patient unfolding. It is miraculous that after such a wise observation the very next thought is inevitably, "What will be?" I look for a way to reconcile my hopes and desires with patient unfolding only to find myself lost, deep in thought again.

early morning
a dog barking
at the wind

The timer beeps. Opening my eyes to the room I find it has brightened. Daybreak has become dawn and is fast becoming day. The neighborhood begins to fill with sounds of people setting into the state of motion that carries them through their days. Car doors slam. Engines turn over. The squeal of tires as someone drives off reveals that even at this early hour people are already late for something.

I bow, pressing my head to the floor. It is not the dirt beneath a giant ficus, but the intention remains the same. I feel my heart loosen as I ring the bell. As it resonates I untangle my legs and begin the motions that will take me through this day. I too am late.

> the chatter of sparrows—
> what will be will be, yet still
> I hope

John Stevenson ✦ United States

opportunity

Alzheimer's—
the word is . . .
kettle

We've been down this road with her sister and I saw how mom always tried to fill in the blanks or to correct her when she said something that made no sense. I vowed to myself I wouldn't do that because I could see it did no good and only made my aunt feel more ashamed. It's been easy enough to keep this vow with aunt Marian but mom is different.

This morning we were looking at pictures on the sideboard when we came to my father's. "He died," she said. "I don't believe you knew him."

Dad died when I was twenty-four, so I was taken by surprise and thus missed an opportunity. Just afterward I realized I could've simply asked, "What was he like?"

Alzheimer's—
I remind her
of her son

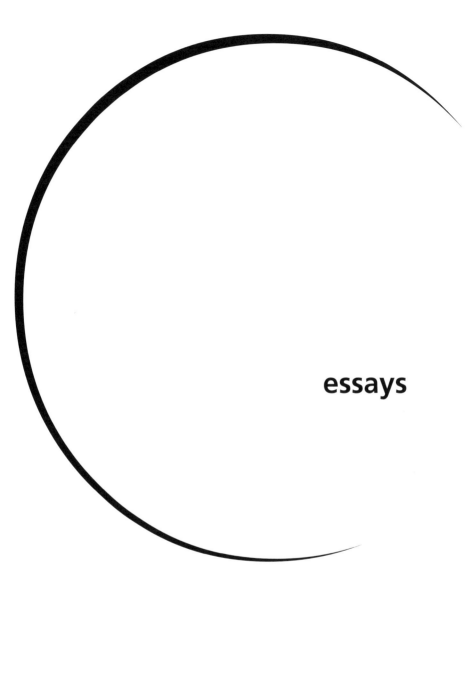

essays

Dee Evetts ✧ United States

The Conscious Eye: Divorce

I am indebted to Tom Painting for suggesting divorce as a theme for this column, and equally to Charles Trumbull for providing an abundance of material culled from his ever-expanding haiku database. Ironically, though all the signs were there, I had no expectation that when I sat down to write this piece I would find myself in the midst of separating from my wife of ten years. The timing of this has added for me an extra significance to many of the poems I have been considering for discussion.

In the process it has been impressed on me just how much strong work there is to be found on this topic. Somewhat ruefully I concluded that this is really not at all surprising. The ending of a significant relationship tends to generate a complex array of feelings, such as anger, disappointment, and grief, typically followed by loneliness or emptiness (not unmixed with intimations of freedom and renewal). These stages are often indelibly linked with particular moments and places and actions.

Profound feelings associated with specific events and images? This sounds like an excellent prescription for haiku composition—and so it proves to be. As a place to start we could hardly do better than to re-examine Alexis Rotella's archetypal

> Discussing divorce
> he strokes
> the lace tablecloth[1]

It would surely be unfair to say that this has inspired many imitations. It is more likely that numerous poets have been impelled to record their experience of *that* conversation—the one in which the unthinkable is not only thought, but put into words. Here are two more examples, by Fred Donovan and George Swede, respectively:

discussing divorce—
my onion chopping
quickens[2]

calmly talking divorce
underfoot the crackle
of fallen leaves[3]

Both of these are evocative enough, yet remain essentially one-dimensional. By comparison, Rotella's poem feels multi-layered and correspondingly more interesting. (We should note in passing that it may or may not refer to the poet's own relationship.) The word "strokes", while conveying something akin to embarrassment or placation, serves also as a reminder of past tenderness, of intimacy lost. Meanwhile the lace tablecloth is suggestive of family ties—if not an heirloom, then something fine that must soon be reckoned among the possessions to be divided. It is easy to see why this poem has been so often republished and anthologized.

Of course there are always antecedents, whether months or years in advance of the pivotal conversation: small cracks in the edifice of marriage.

Divorce? she echoes
I'm not thinking of it.
Thinking of it[4]

This is Ruth Yarrow, giving us a scrap of dialogue

(between the couple, between women friends?—it works either way) that poses the larger question: where does the heretical idea come from? Precisely when does the unthinkable become thinkable?

Among the more painful of circumstances must be the case where one partner has already decided on breaking up while the other still has no inkling of this. Jeff Witkin has expressed this predicament with great poignancy in his

> perennials
> for my wife of thirty years
> . . . not knowing it's over[5]

This appears as the second poem in a collection that chronicles the poet's experience of divorce from first intimations through to the beginnings of acceptance and healing. The above is closely followed by a poem that confirms the partners' disparate viewpoints:

> cold november night—
> she adds another
> reason for divorce[6]

I admire the finely-judged misdirection provided by the second line. The phrase "she adds another" would so often be the prelude to something nurturing ("log to the fire", "dish to the table"). The reader's expectation being nudged in that direction helps to deepen the chill of the last line.

It is obvious that in these few pages I have been able to do no more than introduce this far-reaching topic, one that touches so many lives. I now envisage a series of articles, aiming to encompass successive stages: the process and aftermath of separation, the pangs of child custody, the role of ex-partners and the forming of new relationships. I hope that some readers will send their own best work relating to any of these aspects, or alternatively recommend any noteworthy haiku they may have read.

To conclude with a forward glance, this poem by Jane Reichhold would appear to be located in the very thick of a difficult break-up:

> Mother's Day
> the daughter's call
> about her divorce[7]

The suggestion here, as I read it, is that the daughter is so preoccupied with her own drama that she has overlooked the fact that the day is Mother's Day. Our personal crises tend to drive out the attention and consideration we might usually have for those around us. The poet has achieved a fine balance between humor and compassion, and seems to be saying: this too is human.

---

1. *Frogpond* VI:3
2. *pocket change* (towpath anthology 2000, Winchester, VA: Red Moon Press, 2000)
3. *Almost Unseen: The Selected Haiku of George Swede* (Decatur, IL: Brooks Books, 2000)
4. *Wind Chimes* 8
5. *Beyond Where the Snow Falls*, Enfield CT: Tiny Poems Press, 1997)
6. *ibid.*
7. *A Dictionary of Haiku* (Gualala, CA: AHA Books 1992)

Kai Falkman ✧ Sweden

The Mechanics of Haiku

The Fan

higurashi ya kyu-ni akaruki umi no kata

is a haiku by Issa which R. H. Blyth translates

> The lake
> Is bright over there suddenly:
> A *higurashi* sings.

The *higurashi* is a kind of cicada and in the original poem, as you can see, it opens the poem. This English version of mine shows the correct order of the images:

> A cicada!
> Suddenly it grows light
> over the lake.

When the poet hears the song of the cicada, the light over the lake changes, growing brighter. The *sound* seems to affect the light.

In Blyth's version the air suddenly grows lighter over the lake, after which comes a possible explanation: a *higurashi* is singing. This retrospective explanation is so unclear that readers have to recall the lake before they can alter the first image—the image which portrayed the increasing light objectively rather than subjectively.

117

In the Japanese poem we hear a sound and brightness suddenly spreads over the lake; it is like a *fan* opening up before our eyes. But in Blyth's version the landscape is actually diminished by the arrival of the cicada.

kono michi ya yuku hito nashi ni aki no kure

This is a famous haiku by Basho and Blyth makes of it

An autumn eve;
Along this road
Goes no one.

The mood of desolation and loneliness is apparent already in the first line. The second and third lines reinforce this mood. Where is the surprise, where is the extension of the theme?

The Japanese original, on the other hand, starts with the image of the road. The road may lead anywhere, to fortune or disaster or to neither, in mood it is more or less neutral. It provides a strong 'earth line' which stimulates curiosity and the imagination: where does this road go? Who or what is on it?

The second line provides an answer: there's no one on it. The road becomes empty and desolate.

In the third line the mood darkens into an *autumn evening*. At the same time the road disappears into the trees, swallowed up in the landscape and becoming part of the cosmic cycle of the seasons. Similarly, the mood of human desolation dissolves too; the figure who must be on the road to see that it is empty (poet, reader) also becomes part of the eternal cycle. A picture of universal meaning emerges:

Along this road
goes no one.
Autumn eve.

This poem could also be interpreted more pessimistically: we are all of us alone on the path through life which leads inevitably to death (autumn eve). But even in this interpretation the view is cosmic, which is not in Blyth's version, where the opening image of the autumn evening is never transformed or enhanced with greater symbolic value. In his version the autumn evening remains just an autumn evening.

A few pages later on in his *A History of Haiku*, Blyth makes another attempt :

No-one
Walks this road;
Autumn evening.

But even this translation is not particularly happy. The opening fails to provide an 'earth line'; the inner eye or mind can find no fixed point in *No-one*. In the second line, *no one* acquires a meaning as it is linked to *walks,* but this means that walks assumes too great an importance at the expense of *this road.* No one walks this road; perhaps they always go along it on horseback or in a carriage?

Rather surprisingly, Blyth gives us a third translation in the same volume:

Along this autumn road
Goes no one,
This autumn eve.

This version comes closer to the original, but by calling the road an *autumn road* the later effect of *autumn eve* is diminished.

Let us close this series of discussions by looking at Basho's other famous 'autumn evening' haiku, with Blyth's translation:

kare-eda ni karasu no tomari ken aki no kure

Autumn evening;
A crow perched
On a withered branch.

The first line sets a mood, but the scene lacks precision. In the second and third lines this mood is clarified and the eeriness and transitoriness of an autumn evening are brought into play. We feel the crow, damp, dark. However, true haiku never closes on such a dark and hopeless note. Even in its most melancholy mood we are always left with a glimmer of light, the possibility of a new opening. And so it is in the original version of Basho's poem:

On a withered branch
a crow has landed.
Autumn evening.

Line 1 fills us with the mood of autumn, using concrete detail. In line 2, while the emphasis shifts from the withered state of the branch to the living crow, the mood is reinforced by a symbol of transience and death. Landing *(tomari* implies a dynamic interplay between the silhouettes of branch and crow which is not caught so well in Blyth's *perched.*

The final image, *autumn evening,* is at once concentrated and tensing, but at the same time expansive. We are invited to look beyond the crow on its withered branch and to see whatever else is in our imagination—an autumnul landscape, darkening, perhaps cloudy, sky? Though the forbidding crow and branch remain as points on the earth line, our senses draw away into a landscape where there is still a possibility of light.

120

Caroline Gourlay ✧ Wales

Some Thoughts on the Writing of Haiku and Other Poems

In considering my response to the question do I write haiku in the same way that I write longer poems, I thought it a good moment to ask myself whether or not I believe haiku to be a form of poetry. As regards most aspects of haiku, there are varying opinions on this. In *Traces of Dreams,* Haruo Shirane persuades us that Basho saw himself in the context of the Japanese literary tradition and therefore must have thought of haiku as poetry and himself as a poet. R. H. Blyth on the other hand, maintained that a haiku was not a poem. "Haiku...has little or nothing to do with poetry, socalled, or Zen, or anything else". *(Haiku: Vol. 1, Eastern Culture)* He goes on to say what he does think haiku is: ". . . a way of living, a certain tenderness and smallness of mind that avoids the magnificent . . ." none of which to my mind rules out haiku as poetry. In fact, I believe that it *is* poetry, for if a haiku isn't a poem, what is it? It certainly isn't an epigram, a statement, or an aphorism; neither is its brevity a barrier to its claim to be poetry—several poems that find their way into collections and anthologies are no more than two or three lines long.

That said, it seems that there are comparatively few people who approach the writing of haiku and the writing of longer poems with the same degree of interest or seriousness. Many haiku poets, to give themselves a change, will occasionally write a longer poem but probably don't bother trying to get it published, and we know that some mainstream poets make it their practice to limber up with the writing of haiku in order to get themselves going on what they regard as 'proper' poetry; for them haiku is a means to an end rather than an end in itself.

So, what is the difference between the method employed in the writing of a haiku and that in writing a longer poem? Having talked to several people who do practise both, it would appear that most have no difficulty in working on both simultaneously. I would like to be able to do this, but I find I can't; for some reason when I am focusing on haiku I don't seem able to write longer poems and vice versa. Although I believe that haiku is a poetic form, it is somehow unlike other poetry and consequently my approach for writing it is different; I almost feel that I inhabit different frames of mind, almost different selves, depending on whether I am writing haiku or a longer poem.

As every haiku writer knows, for a haiku to be effective it has to pack its punch in very few syllables—there is no time for an experience, idea or narrative to build up or unfold. The haiku has to be right here, now—indeed it cannot be set in the context of time, for it is instantaneous, fleeting, eternally present. A good haiku must demonstrate the only reality which is the present and will come out of an awareness of the true nature of existence, making connections below the level of rational thought. Three haiku that are good examples of this come to mind—ones that I feel were not consciously thought up, but have come to the writer unbidden:

> Medical reprieve
> wandering the streets
> empty handed   *Ken Jones*

breakfast in silence
both halves of the grapefruit
unsweetened   *David Cobb*

custody battle
a bodyguard lifts the child
to see the snow   *Dee Evetts*

There is nothing contrived or derivative in any of these; they are first hand, authentic. In their different ways all three reveal profound truths about human nature and have a quality that lifts them above the ordinary. Why would a medical *reprieve* leave one 'empty handed'? With the rational mind the opposite would be true; but one knows immediately that it is absolutely right.

Every good haiku points to the here and now, whether it deals with a moment relating to nature, or human nature, or successfully links the two— moments of intense awareness that can only be arrived at during those comparatively rare moments when we are truly living in the present. The writing of haiku is, if not a way of life, a way of seeing. However, we do not always achieve this ideal of fully engaging with the moment; for most of us any ordinary day brings its pressures and preoccupations when all we can do is sit down, knowing that what we attempt will probably be second rate. But that isn't a reason not to write on a daily basis; there are techniques that can be employed, exercises that we can do that will help us to make language work for us. This aspect of working at it applies to the writing both of haiku and longer poems. I have never subscribed to the view that the 'poet' should wait until the spirit moves before sitting down to write. Waiting for 'inspiration' means that it will come less and less often. Writing is a craft and should be practised as such; only if the tools of the trade are kept in good shape is the writer prepared when the Muse does decide to visit.

The brevity of haiku demands a high degree of intensity and every syllable has to be not only the right one, but the *only* one. Maybe the reason that I cannot write longer poems at the same time as I am concentrating on haiku is because when I focus on the latter I build up a kind of 'haiku mind' (or 'haiku no-mind'); I begin to form the habit of living more intensely in the present, of seeing the 'ordinary' as extraordinary. Writing a longer poem demands as much attention and energy as writing haiku, but maybe not in the same way. It requires different skills and, in certain respects, more stamina. In many longer poems the dictates of the form— villanelle, sonnet or whatever—discipline the poet, whereas in haiku the spirit is considered more important than the syllable count. Also, with the writing of longer poems, a familiarity with the subject one is writing about is necessary. Norman McCaig could not have written with such authority on countryside matters if he had not had a deep knowledge and appreciation of the natural world; likewise, Derek Walcott could not have written *Omeros* had he not immersed himself in the Greek myths. No haiku writer needs any such specialised knowledge, just trusts an ability to *see,* to appreciate the moment and record it with accuracy.

One can be more relaxed about writing a longer poem; it gives one greater leeway than a haiku, for the writing of it will probably be spread over a period of anywhere from days, to years. You can meet it in the past, your own and/or the poem's, accompany it through the present and follow it into the future. There is a sense in which a poem is never finished; it can stretch and yawn, venture up alleyways, only to return and change direction if a particular foray proves unsatisfactory. A writer can start a poem, nudged by a phrase or image that takes root in the mind, an idea that might open interesting doors, not knowing how the poem will end or which aspect of the writer's experience or vision it will finally represent. One can leave it and come back to it; so long as it continues to hold one's enthusiasm and remains alive in imagination, it will eventually flower. These kinds of liberties can never be taken with a haiku. If you don't grab the haiku the instant it makes its appearance, the moment is gone, like a lizard leaving only its tail in your hand. With a poem there is more slack, greater room for manoeuvre; you can return to it, alter it, hone it and if you lose the original theme yet keep the impetus, a fresh approach, even after years, will often carry you through to a different but still valid result.

Many feel that the main difference between haiku and mainstream poetry is in the use, or non-use, of metaphor, simile, aphorism and anthropomorphism. There is insufficient space here to deal more than superficially with this topic, but suffice it to say I feel that in these areas there is more of an overlap than is often supposed. The writing of all poetry, haiku or otherwise, depends on using what is appropriate in the given situation rather than in the keeping or breaking of rules. Where anthropomorphism is concerned, I believe that unless used with the greatest subtlety it weakens all poetry and should be avoided. Aphorism in haiku is always inappropriate, telling rather than pointing, working through the intellect rather than the senses. Simile, which can be effective in longer forms, also rarely seems to work in haiku, lessening tension and taking up too many valuable syllables, but metaphor is more complex and used correctly has an important place in all poetry—it is a powerful tool in the hands of any poet and one of the most effective ways of creating meanings on different levels. It is not always appropriate in haiku: the kind of wild, idiosyncratic metaphors that make Sylvia Plath's and Anne Sexton's poetry so vivid and memorable, for instance, would be quite out of place in so short a form since the writer would lose touch with the reader.

Another area in which haiku and the writing of longer poems share common ground is in the extraordinarily difficult business of saying what we really mean, or rather *knowing* what we want to say. So often we think we are clear about what we want to communicate until we pick up the pen, then somehow the words elude us and we find that what we thought was a strong idea or image in our minds is only an intimation. Hunting down what lies behind this vague, yet pressing, reality takes a surprising amount of concentrated energy. It is so much easier to let the mind slide over what it was that first caught our attention and search out something more accessible. But though it might be more accessible and familiar, it will be less interesting, for herein lies the danger of derivative writing and clichés—the easy option. The difference between a strikingly original poem or haiku and a second rate one depends on the integrity of the writer. John Burnside, a poet I greatly admire, has just such an ability to honour the original purpose of the poem; his poems are well worth reading not only for their integrity and individuality but also for their intelligent use of language.

Harold Henderson has said that "haiku is more akin to silence than to words". We know what he means and this statement sums up for me the main difference between it and other forms of poetry. Because haiku is more akin to silence than to words does not mean that it is not a valid form of poem, but it does mean that in some essential way it is different from other forms. In conclusion, I would say that because I perceive this to be an important difference, I can only approach the writing of haiku in a different way from the writing of a longer poem. Perhaps this difference is felt by many poets, even if they are not consciously aware of it, and accounts for the fact that at the moment anyway most tend to write either haiku or longer poems but not both. It remains to be seen which direction haiku will take in the future. If the view that haiku is ". . . evolving . . . into a new genre of short poetry that enables each individual to express something important in a few words" (Ban'ya Natsuishi) supersedes the view of haiku based on the spiritual origins of the classical Japanese haiku— those encompassed in the 13 states of mind considered necessary for the writing of it, then it is almost certain that haiku will become indistinguishable from other forms of poetry. Its brevity, however, will never be in question. More important than having something 'important' to say is having the desire and the ability to say it effectively. With so few syllables in which to do so, this will always challenge the haiku poet in a unique way.

David G. Lanoue ✧ United States

Issa & Buddhism

Historically speaking, the first Buddha became such through an act of meditation. Siddhartha Gautama sat himself down under that fig tree, locked his legs firmly together in a lotus position, and waited. He vowed not to budge from the spot till he attained Supreme Enlightenment. He kept this vow. In the 6th century B.C., in a place in ancient India shaded by what would later be called the Bodhi Tree, the Tree of Wisdom, the man Siddhartha woke up, and Buddha was born.

What he experienced on that day under that tree cannot be expressed or explained in words, according to Nancy Wilson, author of *Buddhism: A Way of Life and Thought*. However, she does her best to describe the experience:

> As a term, enlightenment signifies a direct, dynamic spiritual experience brought about, in the Buddhist view, through the faculty of intuition, a faculty developed and sharpened by such spiritual disciplines as intensive meditation and contemplation. It is a condition beyond the power and pull of "the opposites," a full realization of the universe and the self as one.[1]

Unlike other figures in world religions, Wilson notes, the Buddha's enlightenment did not involve divine intervention. For Gautauma Buddha, Nirvana "lay in the here-and-now [. . .] not in some remote realm or celestial state far beyond one's present existence".[2]

Seeking to duplicate his experience under the Bodhi Tree, the Buddha's followers, especially those of the Zen school, adopted sitting meditation as a central practice. In sitting Zen, one keeps perfectly still, open to that which is, intuiting connection and oneness where ordinary eyes see division and separateness. The first master of haiku, Matsuo Basho, studied Zen and imbued his own art with the sensibilities of that sect. Thanks to Basho, the one-breath poetry of haiku came to demand of its most serious practitioners the same attitude of Gautama Buddha under the Wisdom Tree, one of openness, receptivity, and non-intellectual, intuitive insight. A frog leaps into an old pond, and the poet, attentive to the here-and-now, focuses attention on the simple, wondrous "sound of water," *mizu no oto*. With words he intimates connections that lie beyond words; through language he arrives at pregnant silence.

Issa did not belong to the Zen sect, nor is there evidence that he studied Zen or practiced sitting meditation. However, the particular school where he received his haiku training claimed the legacy of Basho, and sought to emulate him—and so Issa learned to practice and portray a Zen openness to the here-and-now:

daibutsu no hana kara detaru tsubame kana

from the great bronze
Buddha's nose
a swallow![3]

The haiku ends with kana, a particle of emphasis in traditional haiku. Following nouns[4] *kana* has the literal effect of "Ah! Imagine that!" In the present case, the immense statue sneezes out life as a swallow darts from its cavernous nostril, or, as Bob Jones envisions the moment, a whole flock of them "pour forth". Either way, Issa gasps with delight.

In haiku after haiku, this pattern of quiet observance followed by stunning revelation is repeated, and so Issa's poetic method recapitulates the sitting and awakening of Buddha under the Bodhi Tree. Though he makes no claim or even suggests that nirvana waits at the end of his one-breath poems, Issa typically concludes them with insights into the marvel of the ordinary that are much in keeping with the spirit of Buddhist awakening. After which, he trails off into silence, leaving the reader to savor the experience.

yuzen to shite yama wo miru kawazu kana

serene and still
mountain viewing
frog

This haiku appears in *Hachiban nikki* (*Eighth Diary*) in 1813, without prescript, but Issa recopies it six years later in *Oraga haru* (*My Spring*) with a prose preface: "In the summer evening, spreading my straw mat, I call 'Lucky! Lucky!' and soon he comes crawling out from his hiding place in the thicket, enjoying the evening cool just like a person". The editors of Issa's collected works explain that "Lucky" (*fuku*) is a pet name for toads. On its surface the haiku is comic. Someone is sitting "serene and still," looking at a mountain or mountains, but in the end, the moment of insight and surprise, this someone turns out to be a critter: *kawazu kana,* a frog—imagine that! Yet deeper than its humor, the poem and its prescript reveal the oneness of Lucky and Issa. Both enjoy the cool evening air, both gaze at the mountains, and both do so with an attitude of sublime tranquility. Issa describes their common state with the word *yuzen*: *yu*, "boundless calm," and *zen*, "resembling." Frog and poet sit in profound meditation. Lucky the Frog, like Issa, is a Buddhist.

The particle *keri* does for verbs what *kana* does for nouns, providing a final emphasis, in this case for an action rather than a thing, before the aftermath of silence.[5]

ushi mo mo mo to kiri kara detari keri

moo, moo, moo
cows emerge
from the mist

In his translation of this haiku, Blyth imagines one cow in the scene, but I prefer to visualize several. In either case, the climactic word, the focus of attention and delight, is *detari*, to come forth, to emerge. My translation somewhat rearranges Issa's ordering of the images: (1) cows mooing, (2) from mist, (3) they emerge! The miracle of cows in their ponderous bodies materializing from the nothingness of autumn mist is so natural, so ordinary, and yet so astounding.

As has been mentioned, Issa was a Pure Land Buddhist, a devout follower of the Jodoshinshu sect. He concludes his 1819 poetic diary, *Oraga haru* with a description of how trust in the Buddha is a transforming experience:

> Rather than the mouth reciting *namu amida butsu* while weaving a net of greed over the fields, behaving like a long-armed spider, robbing people's sight, a transient wild goose passing through the world; one never again shall possess the heart and mind of one who steals water for "my" rice field. One need not constantly strain to raise one's voice, reciting the *nembutsu*—such is not needed, for the Buddha deigns to protect us. Hence, the so-called great peace of spirit [. . . Thy will be done]!

131

Issa scorns the *nembutsu* chanters who believe that they are somehow in control of their destinies, that by invoking Amida's name their future rebirth in the Pure Land might be assured. Such people, Issa argues, have not moved beyond covetousness, for their desire for personal salvation is as insidious and as spiritually damaging as the greed of a farmer who steals water from a neighbor's field. Those who think to save themselves by chanting the *nembutsu* are as avaricious, Issa claims, as long-armed spiders. In short, they are thieves, since having "long arms" is a Japanese euphemism for kleptomania. They seek to steal that which can only be freely given: the Buddha's salvation. The Pure Land Buddhist cannot "earn" rebirth in the Pure Land any more than a Christian, by personal effort, can earn redemption. No one's arms are that long. In both religious systems, grace is required.

The haiku that follows Issa's salvation treatise poetically expresses the theme of submission:

tomokaku mo anata makase no toshi no kure

come what may
trusting in the Buddha
the year ends

For human beings, according to Issa, a childlike faith in Amida's power is required:

namu namu to meigetsu ogamu kodomo kana

"Praise 'Mida!"
in harvest moonlight
a child prays

Just as the nembutsu is a joyous prayer of gratitude for Amida Buddha's grace, poetry becomes a form of prayer for Issa, a celebration of Nature. When he opens his palms to catch the flitting-down flakes of snow, he does so with reverence:

tenohira e hara-hara yuki no furi ni keri

to my open palms
snow flitting
down

Just as one cannot demand salvation or control Amida's grace, Issa approaches Nature with open palms and grateful acceptance. Haiku is his praise-song for blooming flowers, shining moon, fellow creatures, wind, rain, snow, and all wonders of the universe, received, in the moment of poetic insight, as precious and sacred gifts. For Issa, prayer and poetry are one.

When one sits, waits, and watches—like Gautama Buddha under the Bodhi Tree, the universe reveals itself, yielding insight and revelation. Though he was not a contemplative Buddhist, his poetic attitude was shaped by this tradition. The Pure Land Buddhism to which he did subscribe convinced him to surrender all calculating efforts, both in the quest for salvation and for the next poem. With joyful trust, Issa opened himself to the Other Power, and wrote.

hito shizuku atama nade keri hikigaeru

a raindrop falls
he rubs his head
toad

•

NOTES

1. This paper was delivered at the Global Haiku Festival hosted by Millikin University, April 16, 2000; it appeared in Modern Haiku Vol. 32, No. 1 (Winter-Spring, 2001): 35-40.

2. English translations of the haiku in this essay have been published (2000) on my "Haiku of Kobayashi Issa" website: <www.xula.edu/~dlanoue/issa/>.

3. In rare cases, *kana* follows verbs in Issa's haiku; for example: *yama-garasu orega tsugiki wo warau kana:*

> the mountain crow
> laughs at the branch
> I grafted

Here, *kana* follows *warau* ("laughs"). However, *kana* more typically follows and emphasizes nouns.

4. *Keri*, I've been told, is an archaic past tense verb ending—literally. However, its cadence and effect in oral recitation make it analogous to *kana* in that it highlights and brings poetic emphasis to the action.

WORKS CITED

Blyth, R. H. *Haiku.* Tokyo: Hokuseido, 1949-1952; rpt. 1981-1982 [reset paperback edition]. 4 vols.

Issa. *Issa zensh®.* Nagano: Shinano Mainichi Shimbunsha, 1976-1979. 9 vols.

Jones, Bob. "Seasonality." Modern Haiku 27, No. 3 (1996): 47-50.

Ross, Nancy Wilson. *Buddhism: A Way of Life and Thought.* New York: Vintage Books, 1981.

H. F. Noyes ✧ Greece

The Way of Haiku

Haiku is surely the most elusive form of poetry. Every time one tries to define it, the "rule" is broken in the same week by one of our best haiku poets. But art in all its forms is mysteriously elusive to some degree. Artists are always trying to convey the *how* of their success, and their explanations are generally of little help to the beginner. What is most vital is that we expose ourselves to the *spirit* of the art form.

The spirit of haiku lies most of all in its simplicity and in its selflessness. Both are a *way* of life requiring real commitment and depth of understanding. The simple, and the plain and ordinary, are quite different. One learns from the Japanese haiku that simplicity is characterized by a feel for the flow of life and the harmony of nature, which translation often fails to find. Here we have one of Shiki's plainest haiku:

A stream
flowing through the town
and the willows along it.

Yet in Japanese, the flow and the euphony are inescapable:

machi naka o ogawa nagaruru yanagi kana

The greatest secret of haiku writing is to listen to the voice of things, to let nature speak for itself. Just listen to the woody, watery, sounds!

Another secret is to allow the haiku moment to choose *you*, rather than, with our near-inescapable duality, trying to choose the moment yourself. The mind is the great interferer. tony suraci, editor of the 1980s magazine *old pond*, called mentality the "only barrier:

> It's always unsubstantial, unalive, unactual, unreal and untrue—it can never substitute for anything alive.

And our thought is not rooted in eternity, as is the fleeting haiku moment. It's fully claimed by time—a stranger to tunelessness.

Our ego is concerned with means to an end. Nothing could be farther removed from the spirit of haiku. The ego-self is only an illusion, in any case, as Buddhism has made very clear. Yes, our individuality is expressed, as in *all* forms of art. But the haiku is in no respect primarily a means of self-expression. The haiku way is a path on which the followers shed the ego just as naturally as a snake sheds its skin or a butterfly emerges freed of its cocoon. We are not intended to live our lives cocooned off from nature and reality, as if the self were a virtual prison. The natural self, the self that is one with all of nature, does not see itself as subject and all else as mere object. Basho warned us that if you and the object of your observation in the haiku moment have not become one, the feeling you express cannot be natural, and your haiku will be a mere imitation of life.

Let us also consider what is noteworthy, according to the haiku tradition. Let us not make the mistake of trying to say something unusual, something original. Robert Spiess has pointed out that the desire for novelty for novelty's sake is strongly rejected in the haiku tradition. "Originality," he says, "does not mean novelty, but direct contact with things in their original nature. It is the *suchness* of things that is vital."

In conclusion, I would like to offer my two favorite quotes from Spiess's "Speculations", as I feel they offer special insight into the spirit of haiku. "In being a momentary interruption of silence," he observes, "haiku actually are affirming the primacy of silence." They emerge from the silence, only to re-enter it a moment later. Eric Amann called haiku the wordless poem because it is as much what is not said and cannot be said—that comes through to the reader, as the actual words the poet has used. My second quote reminds us that haiku are never mere description, never mere reports of what our senses convey. They reflect the inner eye, the inner ear, our feelings "from the bottom of the heart." He says:

> Haiku poets write from the heart and only tangentially or peripherally by the mind; for the light of the latter, like that of the moon, only exists because of the light of the heart, the sun.

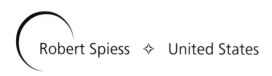

Robert Spiess ✧ United States

A Certain Open Secret about Haiku

In being here today the wisdom of Ajahn Chah comes to mind: "Do not speak unless you can improve on silence." However, as haiku is essentially the briefest of poetry, it comes closest to silence, and perhaps your compassionate nature will allow me to forego for a short while the sanctity of silence.

Preliminary to the main subject, "A Certain Open Secret about Haiku," I would like to mention that a haiku is not a brief bit of prose, scientific account, journalistic report, intellective comment, aphorism, epigram or the like. It is a unique mode of poetry with characteristics and attributes that most poems do not have, particularly in the manner in which they are combined in haiku. I shall touch on some of these attributes.

A haiku does not exceed a breath's length. The reason for this probably stems from the fact that a deeply felt *moment of awareness* of an event-experience can last only this long. During this moment of pure awareness our intellect is in abeyance, and we simply are experiencing the moment in the depth of our psyche. In one of his many books of translations of Japanese haiku, R. H. Blyth wrote: "A haiku is a flash of illumination in which we enter into things."

The purpose, then, of the haiku poet is to memorialize this moment, which may be one that is recalled from memory, by exteriorizing it through language. This can be accomplished only by a poem that is very brief, and specifically through the genius of the traditional aesthetics that are the foundation of haiku.

Genuine haiku do not express ideas but put forward sensory images that evoke intuition or insight into the suchness or essence of entities. Therefore, they are not cognitive, ratiocinative, analytical, or examples of mere cause and effect. They can be said to be created not from our head but from the body's center of gravity—or from what all traditional Teachings affirm, namely, that the seat of wisdom is not in the head but in the heart. Five thousand years ago a person in Egypt carved hieroglyphs on a slab of stone that translate as: "When the eyes see, the ears hear, and the nose breathes, they report to the heart. It is the heart that brings forth every issue and the tongue that repeats the thoughts of the heart." (This stone is in the British Museum and is known as Stele Nr. 797.) Haiku poets will not go astray in holding to the belief among the ancients that the brain is merely the organ for cooling the blood

Aspects of nature usually are included in haiku. It would not appear that haiku's use of natural objects as its foundation is more or less by happenstance. Rather, some sort of conscious or nonconscious intention is involved, for natural objects are the best means of expression of that which guides humankind toward egoless self-integration and comprehension of one's essential beingness. We are immersed in and linked with the all-encompassing, natural universe. The accomplished Japanese woman poet, Chiyo, said: "A haiku must be the expression of inner feelings totally devoid of ego." And Dogen, the 13th century founder of Japanese Soto Zen, wrote: "To forget the ego is to be illuminated by all things." But this does not mean that personal pronouns, such as "I" or "me" are not to be used in haiku, though in Japanese haiku personal pronouns are rare. This stricture against inclusion of the self in haiku just indicates that one's self when it is a part of haiku generally should be well in the background or almost hidden—much like in those wonderful landscapes of Chinese artists where we must look ever so closely to find a very small human figure rounding a cliff on a narrow path, or perhaps only an indication of a person, as by a bit of the prow of a boat peeping from a growth of reeds.

As most of us live in cities we may believe that we have little opportunity for finding nature. But nature does not have to be "wild nature". A couple of haiku about nature that a city dweller could come upon:

the city bus stop—
through the opened door a caw
    of a winter crow

white peony—
an ant draws its forelegs
along a feeler

In reference to the things of nature, each entity is wonderful in itself. In haiku it exceedingly seldom needs the trappings of simile, metaphor, personification, anthropomorphism, and never of prettiness or sentimentality.

Basho, "the spiritual founder of haiku" (R. H. Blyth) and the most eminent of haiku poets, said, "Go to the pine if you want to learn about the pine, or to the bamboo if you want to learn about the bamboo. And in doing so, you must leave your subjective preoccupation with yourself. Otherwise you impose yourself on the object and do not learn. Your poetry issues of its own accord when you and the object have become one, when you have plunged deep enough into the object to see something like a hidden glimmering there. However well phrased your poetry may be, if your feeling is not natural—if the object and yourself are separate—then your poetry is not true poetry but merely your subjective counterfeit."

However, these words do not imply that a haiku is to be simply objectivity, per se, just bare facts, but that the poet's choice of words, their associative qualities in relation to each other and to the haiku's entities, their cadence, music, must evoke depth of feeling in the hearer of the haiku. Therefore, haiku do not explain or overtly tell the poet's feelings; they hint at or suggest. With haiku the part is greater than the whole. As R. H. Blyth puts it: "The whole is the whole, but the half is infinite." And the perception of that unknown writer of 3rd century China is applicable to haiku: "The mind of heaven loves not what is too complete."

Now for the open secret—in the nine-volume English-language *Kodansha Encyclopedia of Japan* the entry for haiku states in part:

From the point of view of formal technique, the most vital element (after brevity) in the creation of haiku-like expression is the technique of cutting. What this involves is the introduction of a caesura after either the first or second metrical unit so that the poem is cut into two sections. . . . In English the effect is roughly equivalent to a line break punctuated by a colon, long dash or ellipsis.

Cutting is vital to haiku expression because the cut divides the poem into two parts and forces the reader to relate or reconcile these two parts. This struggle to intuit or grasp the poetic association between the two images represents the heart of haiku complexity.

> . . . the successful use of cutting involves three conditions. First, the two sections must be sufficiently distinct and disassociated from each other: *i.e.* in terms of imaginative distance they must not be too near each other. Second, these sections must be related to each other in a manner that precludes total mystification: i.e. they must not be too far apart. Third, the relationship between the two sections must be two-sided: in other words, the first section must enhance the appreciation of the second, and the second section must enhance the appreciation of the first. The internal comparison must be reciprocal.

Note that the definition says that the two sections must not be too near each other. This rules out cause and effect between the two parts, as cause and effect is about as near to each other as can be achieved. However, cause and effect *within* one of the two parts is acceptable. Also, the word "image" was used. In haiku, "image" does not mean only a visual image, but images presented by all our senses. Often the use of different images by different senses in a haiku makes for a more effective haiku.

What is being described is juxtaposition of entities or parts in a haiku. *Webster's Third New International Dictionary* defines juxtaposition as: "The art or instance of placing two or more objects in a close spatial or ideal relation." Please note two important aspects of this definition: the word "art" and the phrase "ideal relation." Haiku is a poem, and a poem is art. And "ideal relation" is important because the juxtaposition of just any objects will not necessarily result in an ideal or genuine haiku. It is interesting that the Japanese word for "juxtaposition" is *toriawase*, literally meaning "putting different things together."

Why does the juxtaposition of two entities in a haiku make it more evocative and aesthetically appreciated than does one entity, even if it is elaborated upon? Isak Dinesen (Countess Karen von Blixen) has a passage in *Shadows on the Grass* that is very applicable to haiku: "In order to form and make up a Unity, in particular a creative unity, the individual components must needs be of different natures, they should even be in a sense contrasts. Two homogeneous units will never be capable of forming a whole, or their whole at its best will remain barren."

In the book *Matsuo Basho,* the author, Makoto Ueda, has several passages that refer to Basho's use of juxtaposition. One of them refers to the development of Basho's haiku style: "Basho now began to juxtapose disparate objects not so much for the shock effect as to create a specific mood or sensation which could not otherwise be evoked."

And Basho is recorded as saying (I do not have the source): "Haiku is a matter of juxtaposition. A person who can bring two elements together and do it well is a skillful poet."

In the *Kodansha* quotation the word "cutting" is used. In Japanese there is the word *kireji,* usually translated as "cutting word" or sometimes as "pause word". *Kireji* are words or suffixes used in Japanese for various purposes, such as to hint at or to express certain affective states of the poet, or to act in a punctuation-like capacity. As Joan Giroux suggests in her book *The Haiku Form,* ". . . it would seem that English punctuation, with its fine nuances, would adequately substitute for *kireji.* An explanation of the shades of meaning indicated by the semicolon, the colon, the linking dash, the exclamation mark and suspension points reveals their value in haiku."

The following excerpt from an article on *kireji* would appear to have value for English-language haiku poets. It is from Professor Tsutomu Ogata's

143

article "Essentials for Writing and Appreciating Haiku." It appears in his *The Cyclopedia of Interpretation and Appreciation of Haiku* (Obunsha Co.) I thank Ryosuke Suzuki for his translation of this excerpt that he sent me in a letter.

> Why did haiku writers start to write verses set apart by means of *kireji?* In order to find an answer, you have to think of the origin of haiku: the beginning part of renga (linked verses). In renga writing, the beginning part should be deep and great as it is the verse which leads the following part to a world of changes and developments. For that purpose, writers had to find something special since the length of the verse was limited. . . . Thus they invented *kireji,* and by cutting the verse apart they tried to produce a silent interval just after the *kireji.* They sometimes succeeded in making readers sense various feelings out of *the space of nonexpression,* or the silent interval. It is, in other words, a new way to express various emotions beyond ordinary experience.

Juxtaposition also has been linked to the two poles in an electrical circuit, in that when the positive and negative poles are brought into proximity a spark jumps across the interval. So is it in haiku: when there is effective juxtaposition a spark of intuition can result.

Let us now look at some haiku in which effective juxtaposition enhances our appreciation of them through our felt-depth, insight or intuition of the now-moment of awareness that the authors experienced. The first is by Roberta Stewart:

Evening bells . . .
shimmer of green tomatoes
in the padre's garden.

In this haiku several elements simultaneously juxtapose. A harmony results from the tension and interplay between the juxtaposed aspects. There is a compound relation between the bells and tomatoes: one is made by humans, the other is natural; one mineral and the other is vegetable. Yet there is a certain similarity to their shape, and also the bells are hard and the tomatoes, being still green, are also relatively hard. In this compound juxtaposition there is a relation or harmony set up between two senses, hearing and sight. The sound of the bells and the shimmer of light reflected from the glossy green tomatoes interplay; they are distinct from each other, yet their effects on us are rather similar. The shimmer is qualitatively the same as the sound of the bells; both have vibrational features that make them akin. Each enhances our appreciation of the other.

There also is juxtaposition or linkage of the first and third lines through the padre (who may or may not be physically present). The padre belongs to both the bells and the garden, to the spiritual and the natural, to nourishment of the soul and nourishment of the body. And just as the greenness of the tomatoes implies later fulfillment, the sound of the bells suggests or invites one to another kind of fulfillment on another plane of beingness.

Of course this interpretation is intellective, even somewhat analytical; but when one becomes acquainted with haiku the aura, as it were, of haiku affects our psyche without need for such explanations.

Janine Beichman, in her book *Masaoka Shiki*, has this translation of a haiku by Shiki:

old garden—
she empties a hot-water bottle
under the moon

Dr. Beichman states:

> The overt content of this poem is indeed simple: someone (unspecified, but one might imagine Shiki's mother or sister) is pouring out the water from a hot-water bottle into an old garden lit up by the moon. Yet, there is more to it than that. The poem juxtaposes a conventionally beautiful object (the moon) with a banal, everyday one (an invalid's hot-water bottle) against the background of an old garden . . . Although the two images are opposite in their association . . . they become complementary opposites, each highlighting the other: as the moon reveals the hot-water bottle on a literal level . . . so the hot-water bottle, on a figurative level, sets off the beauty of the moon by its own banality. Additional associations are possible . . . The moonlight is being reflected in the water poured from the hot-water bottle and the moon and the water are united in a fusion of light and liquidity.

> Or, again, one may take the hot-water bottle as shorthand for the invalid who used it, that is, Shiki himself, and pursue yet another train of association: the moon will go on after both garden and the invalid are gone. Yet here, as the moon and the water from the bottle are, for a moment, one, so too the invalid, by extension, knows a moment of immortality, of respite, from his own mortality. This, finally, is the meaning of the poem. The tawdry mortality of the hot-water bottle and of the invalid who depends on it is seen for a moment in the light of immortality and beauty.

Here is a haiku by Dan McKinley. It carries the title "Viet Nam War Memorial":

Not one day, these
Cherry blossoms in the rain;
Wet black monument

Let us look at some of its characteristics that make it such a fine haiku. In it there is the juxtaposition of a man-made object of stone that stands in contrast to the natural object of soft cherry blossoms. The monument is black and the cherry petals are white and pink. They are linked by the rain that falls equally on both.

Just as the rain does not let the cherry blossoms flower for their full time, so the monument with its many thousands of names symbolizes the death by war that did not allow these scores of thousands of human beings to live out more of the years that would have been allotted to them. And as we feel a sense of poignancy at the untimely falling of the petals, we feel deep grief at the loss of so many persons who also fell untimely.

For the final example please permit me to use one of my own haiku which sometimes has been anthologized, but the interpretation of it is by Dr. J. P. Trammell of the Kentucky State University System. In the haiku the word "stringer" is used and refers to a cord that is threaded through the mouth and a gill opening of a fish that has been caught, is lowered into the water and one end is fastened to the pier or side of the boat.

becoming dusk—
the catfish on the stringer
swims up and down

"The poet summons a response quite beyond the conventional: we *empathize* with a *catfish*. The ominous approach of dusk finds the catfish, often a nocturnal feeder, captive in its own element. Encoding draws it to deeper water, as it 'swims up and down,' following a futile, ancient directive quite insufficient for solving its present dilemma. Because of the adroit juxtaposition of logically unrelated images, we empathize with the fish and suffer the constraints of its captivity. Later we may realize that, through empathy and intuition, we affirmed our kinship with all living things compelled toward liberty and life in the ever-present face of restriction and death."

A few words in conclusion: As all entities in the universe are interconnected, as both traditional Buddhism and modern quantum mechanics inform us, poets can incorporate this verity into their haiku. By using juxtaposition they can evoke in their readers and hearers heightened awareness, felt-depth, insight and intuition of aspects of life and the world around them—aspects that may have been overlooked or superficially considered too mundane to be of interest, but which may be marvelously interlinked.

Thank you.

(Presented at the 50th Anniversary convention of the Wisconsin Fellowship of Poets, June 10, 2000, Green Lake Convention Center, Green Lake, Wisconsin.)

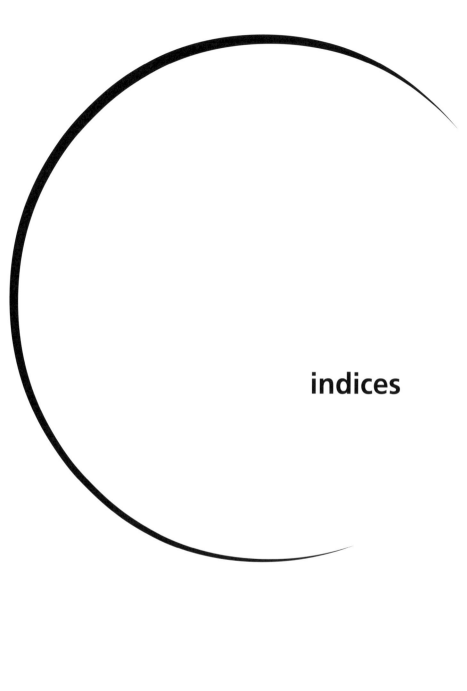

indices

index of authors

151

acknowledgments

Addiss—"late autumn" *Haiku Canada Newsletter* 15:1; **ai li**—"talk of divorce" *RAW NervZ VI:3*; **Akio**—"The snow on a cedar mountain" *Ginyu Anthology 2001*; **aksnes**—"empty corner" *The Heron's Nest* II:12; **Alexander**—"abandoned house" *Frogpond* XXIV:2; **Amor**—"A moonlit night" *Frogpond* XXIV:2; **an'ya**—"After its first flight" Hackett 2001; **Aoyagi**—"Independence Day" *Frogpond* XXIV:3; **Baker**—"breast self-examination" Drevniok 2001; **Barton**—"moving day" HPNC 2000; **Batz**—"April sunrise" *Modern Haiku* XXXII:2; **Better**—"heading into the sunset" *tundra* 2; **Billingsley**—"suddenly" *Snapshots* 7; **Board**—"fiftieth birthday" *The Pianist's Nose*; **Borne**—"in the casket room" *The Pianist's Nose*; **Bond**—"canyon" *Agniewska's Dowry* 12; **M. Brooks**—"new hammock" *Modern Haiku* XXXII:1, "crescent moon" *The Heron's Nest* III:5, "withering end" Mainichi Daily News Contest 2001; **R. Brooks**—"moonrise" *Modern Haiku* XXXII:1, "moonrise" *tundra* 2; **Brydges-Jones**—"arm in plaster" *Frogpond* XXIV:3; **Buckley**—"the ebb and flow" *Blithe Spirit* 10:4; **Chang**—"back at camp" *The Heron's nest* 2:12, "Refrigerator" *American Haibun & Haiga* 2; **Clausen**—"in her sleep" *bottle rockets* 2:2; **D. Cobb**—"the trees move" *Presence* 14, "Down Epiphany Way" *Haiku Spirit* 20; **K. Cobb**—"scraping frost" *Acorn* 6; **crook**—"mid-autumn" *Frogpond* XXIV:1; **Cross**—"dinner alone" *Haiku-kai* III; **Codrescu**—"Towards the Mountain Temple" *American Haibun & Haiga* 2; **Currier**—"at my father's grave" *Modern Haiku* XXXII:3; **Dahl**—"empty cabin" *Snapshots* Calendar 2000; **Day**—"cold snap" *RAW NervZ* VI:3; **Detheridge**—"on the country road" *Blithe Spirit* 11:2; **Detrick**—"public garden" *The Pianist's Nose*; **Dolphy**—"All Saints' Day" *Blithe Spirit* 11:1; **Donleycott**—"30th reunion" *Frogpond* XXIV:2; **Dulleghan**—"searching the cupboard" *Blithe Spirit* 11:1; **Dunphy**—"Facing the Wall" *American Haibun & Haiga* 2; **Elliott**—"Hiking by full moon" *hummingbird* 12:1, "Through the silence" *Modern Haiku* XXXII:1; **Escareal**—"Talons in the Chimney" *RAW NervZ* VI:4; **A. Evans**—"Winder 1950" *Presence* 14; **J. Evans**—"Vigil" *American Haibun & Haiga* 2; **Evetts**—"store window", "retuning" both *The Pianist's Nose* "The Conscious Eye: Divorce" *Frogpond* XXIV:2; **Falkman**—"The Mechanics of Haiku" *Blithe Spirit* 11:2; **Fessler**—"closing time" *Modern Haiku* XXXIII:3; **Forrester**—"winter afternoon" *Frogpond* XXIV:2; **Fraticelli**—"Two Swans" *Haiku Canada Newsletter* 14:2; **Fuhringer**—"changing light" *tundra* 2; **Gallagher**—"a hairline crack" Hackett 2001; **B. George**—"making change" *Modern Haiku* XXXII:1; **G. George**—"Arizona" *American Haibun & Haiga* 2; **Gierat**—"approaching storm" *The Heron's Nest* III:5; **Gilli**—"divorce papers" *Acorn* 6, "autumn wind" *Modern Haiku* XXXII:2, "Talons in the Chimney" *RAW NervZ* VI:4; **L. Gorman**—"exam silence" *South by Southeast* 7:3; "the quiet graveyard" *Frogpond* XXIV:1; **M. Gorman**—"silent car ride" *Frogpond* XXIV:3; **gordon**—"drinking tea" *tundra* 2; **Gourlay**—"below the door" *Frogpond* XXIV:1, "Some Thoughts on the Writing of Haiku and Longer Poems" *Blithe Spirit* 11:1; **Gross**—"snowed in" *Acorn* 6; **Hall**—"indian summer" *Acorn* 6, "January 3rd" *Frogpond* XXIV:2, "Protective Coloration" *American Haibun &N Haiga* 2; **Hardenbrook**—"end of winter" *Modern Haiku* XXXII:3; **Hardy**—"straight road ahead" *Presence* 14; **Hayashi**—"Breaking" *Ginyu Anthology 2001*; **Heinrich**—"first contraction" *Frogpond* XXIV:3; **Hewitt**—"newly pregnant" *Presence* 15; **houck**—"separating fog" *Frogpond* XXIV:2; **Jones**—"Aging address book" *Blithe Spirit* 11:1, "Autumn Gothick" *Presence* 14; **Kacian**—"just now" *The Heron's Nest* III:2, "the melon splits" "sundown" *Upstate Dim Sum* 2, "Every Thanksgiving" *American Haibun & Haiga* 2, "a long trip" *Modern Haiku* XXXII:1, "in the heart" Midwest Haibun Contest 2001; **Kelly**—"light snowfall" *The Heron's Nest* 3:4; **Ketchek**—"Lunar Eclipse" *American Haibun & Haiga* 2; **Kilbride**—"day after diagnosis" *Frogpond* XXIV:2; **Krestova**—"guests gone" *Frogpond* XXIV:1; **Kusch**—"missed the train" *Frogpond* XXIV:3; **Lanoue**—"Issa and Buddhism" *Modern Haiku* XXXII:1; **Lifshitz**—"alone" *Mayfly* 30, "land's end" Henderson 2001; **Lilly**—"A warm breeze" *Modern Haiku* XXXII:1, "Cold autumn dusk" *Presence* 15; **Lippy**—"a cricket" *Acorn* 6; **Lohnes**—"Two Swans" *Haiku Canada Newsletter* 14:2; **Louvière**—"first light" *Modern Haiku* XXXII:1; **Lyles**—"Talons in the Chimney" *RAW NervZ* VI:4; **m.**—"a coyote" *Acorn* 6, "Indian summer" *Haiku-kai* III; **Mainone**—"all around" *Frogpond* XXIV:2; **Mason**—"argument at dinner" *Frogpond* XXIV:3; **Mena**—"snow mixes with rain" *The Heron's Nest* III:4; **Meyers**—"church exit" *Haiku Canada Newsletter* 15:1; **Missias**—"reading the poems" *Modern Haiku* XXXII:1, "veterans' cemetery" *Frogpond* XXIV:2, "holding her hand" *Snapshots* 7; **Moore**—"funeral procession" *The Heron's Nest* II:1; **Morden**—"shortlisting" *tundra* 2; **Mountain**—"just enough rain" *South by Southeast* 8:2; **Naia**—"heat wave" *Haiku-kai* III; **Ness**—"her dead mother's room" *Acorn* 6, "Alzheimer's ward" *Penumbra* 2001, "vacation over" *The Way of Haiku* *Presence* 14; **Owen**—"her estate" *Modern Haiku* XXXII:1, "prostate exam" Brady 2001, "summer wind" *Agniewska's Dowry* 12; **Ower**—"lovers on the beach" *South by Southeast* 8:2; **Painting**—"family plot" *Frogpond* XXIV:2, "solicitation" *RAW NervZ* VI:3; **Patchel**—"midnight stars" *Haiku-kai* III, "spring fever" *Penumbra* 2001, "bitter cold" *Frogpond* XXIV:2; **Paul**—"a train delayed" *Snapshots* 7; **Peruzzi**—"deep summer" *The Heron's Nest* II:12; **Preston**—"hospice visit" New Zealand Poetry Society Haiku Contest 2001; **Prime**—"mending his fence" *Presence* 13; **Pupello**—"blustery wind" *The Pianist's Nose*; **Ramsey**—"afternoon light" *tundra* 2; **Ristow**—"marginal" *bottle rockets* 3:1; **Robeck**—"back from the PO" *Frogpond* XXIV:3, "winter waves" *The Heron's Nest* II:1; **Rogers**—"birthday snow" *Modern Haiku* XXXII:2; **Rohrig**—"Visit to the Mall" *Modern Haiku* XXXII:3; **Ross**—"early spring" *Frogpond* XXIV:2, "dense rains clouds" *Modern Haiku* XXXII:1, "morning fog" *Frogpond* XXIV:3; **Rutter**—"in the next fitting room" *Frogpond* XXIV:2; **Sanfield**—"$200 a night" *Modern Haiku* XXXII:3; **Scotellaro**—"as she talks of aging" *RAW NervZ* VI:4; **Scott**—"still no word" *Frogpond* XXIV:2; **Semimaru**—"The son of God" *Ginyu Anthology*; **Spiess**—"A Certain Open Secret about Haiku" *Modern Haiku* XXXII:1; **Stefanac**—"communion wafer" *RAW NervZ* VII:3; **Steinberg**—"winter rain" *Frogpond* XXIV:2, "haibun" *Frogpond* XXIV:2; **J. Stevenson**—"last piece" *Starfish* Spring 2001, "hazy moon" *RAW NervZ* VI:3, "tax return" *Upstate Dim Sum* 2, "opportunity" *RAW NervZ* VI:3; **R. Stevenson**—

"memorial gun" *Haiku Canada Newsletter* 14:2; **Takiguchi**—"moonless night" *Haiku-kai* III; **Tann**—"hotel room" "eye exam" *Upstate Dim Sum* 2; **Tarquinio**—"sent back out" *The Heron's Nest* III:4; **Tasnier**—"recalling the days" *RAW NervZ* VII:3; **Thompson**—"a small white church" *Modern Haiku* XXXII:1, "steady rain" *Frogpond* XXIV:2; **Tico**—"Thanksgiving" *RAW NervZ* VI:4; **van den Heuvel**—"a drop of water" *The Pianist's Nose*, "deep snow" *bottle rockets* 2:2, "the rusted paperclip" *Paperclips*; **Vayman**—"forest path" *Frogpond* XXIV:2; **Walker**—"wearing the suit" *Haiku Spirit* 20; **Ward**—"heat waves" Henderson 2001, "wind shift" *RAW NervZ* VII:1; **Watt**—"'Zen for Beginners'" *Presence* 14; **Welch**—"the silence between us" *Modern Haiku* XXXII:1; **A. Williams**—"darkness gathers" *Snapshots* 7; **P. Williams**—"five days later" *RAW NervZ* VII:3; **Wilson**—"an open book" *Acorn* 6; **Winke**—"Amtrak depot" *bottle rockets* 2:2; **Yamagishi**—"On the chair" *Ginyu Anthology 2001*; **Yoshida**—"Man will lean" *Ginyu Anthology 2001*; **Zackowitz**—"unseasonable heat" *The Heron's Nest* III:5; **Zorman**—"dry laundry" *Frogpond* XXIV:1.

cited sources

Books:

Ginyu Anthology 2001, ed. Ban'ya Natushishi (Ginyu Press, Fujimi, Japan: 2001).
Paperclipa, ed. Michael Dylan Welch (Press Here, Foster City CA: 2001).
The Pianist's Nose ed. Spring Street Haiku Group (self-published, New York: 2001) .
stone frog: American Haibun & Haiga Volume 2 ed. Jim Kacian & Bruce Ross (Red Moon Press, Winchester VA: 2001).

Periodicals:

Acorn (ed. A. C. Missias, P.O. Box 186, Philadelphia PA 19105 USA)
Agniewska's Dowry (ed. Marek Lugowski, 5445 N Sheridan 3003, Chicago IL 60640 USA)
Blithe Spirit (ed. Colin Blundell, Longolm, East Bank, Wingland, Sutton Bridge, Spalding, Lincs, PE12 9YS, UK)
bottle rockets (ed. Stanford M. Forrester, PO Box 290691, Wethersfield CT 06129 USA)
Frogpond (ed. Jim Kacian, PO Box 2461, Winchester VA 22604-1661 USA)
Haiku Canada Newsletter (ed. LeRoy Gorman, 51 Graham West, Napanee, Ontario K7R 2J6 Canada)
Haiku Spirit (ed. Sean O'Connor, 32 Thornville Avenue, Kilbarrack, Dublin 5 Ireland)
Heron's Nest, The (ed. Christopher Herold, 816 Taft St., Port Townsend WA 98368 USA)
Hummingbird (ed. Phyllis Walsh, PO Box 96, Richland Center WI 53581 USA)
Mayfly (ed. Randy Brooks, 4634 Hale Drive, Decatur IL 62526 USA)
Modern Haiku (ed. Robert Spiess, PO Box 1752, Madison WI 53701 USA)
Presence (ed. Martin Lucas, 12 Grovehall Avenue, Leeds LS11 7EX, England, UK)
RAW NerVZ (ed. Dorothy Howard, 67 Court Street, Aylmer (QC) J9H 4M1 Canada)
Snapshots (ed. John Barlow, PO Box 35, Sefton Park, Liverpool, L17 3EG, England, UK)
South by Southeast (ed. Steve Addis *et. al..*, RC Box 93, 28 Westhampton Way, Richmond VA 23173 USA)
Starfish (ed. Irene Zahava, 307 W. State Street, Ithaca NY 14850 USA)
tundra (ed. Michael Dylan Welch, PO Box 4014, Foster City CA 90044 USA)
Upstate Dim Sum (ed. Route 9 Haiku Group, PO Box 122, Nassau NY 12123 USA)

Contests:

The Betty Drevniok Haiku Contest 2001 (Haiku Canada)
The Gerald Brady Senryu Contest 2001 (Haiku Society of America)
Haiku Poets of Northern California Haiku Contest 2001
Haiku-kai III(World Haiku Club)
The Harold G. Henderson Haiku Contest 2001 (Haiku Society of America)
The James W. Hackett Haiku Competition 2001 (British Haiku Society)
Mainichi Daily News Yearly Haiku Contest 2001
Midwest Poetry Review Haibun Contest 2001
New Zealand Poetry Society Haiku Contest 2001
Penumbra Haiku Contest 2001 (*Penumbra* Magazine)
Snapshots Calendar Haiku Contest 2001 (Snapshots Press)

154

The RMA Editorial Staff

Jim Kacian (1996-2001) is a co-founder of the World Haiku Association, editor of *Frogpond*, and owner of Red Moon Press.

Dimitar Anakiev (2000-1) is a co-founder of the World Haiku Association, and recipient of the Medal of Franz Kafka in 2000.

Jan Bostok (1996-2001) retiring with this issue, has found editing RMA to be one of her most rewarding and enjoyable projects.

Tom Clausen (1996-2001) works in a library at Cornell University and lives with his family in the house where he grew up.

Ellen Compton (1996-2001) is a freelance writer with a background in visual and theatre arts, and a deep love for the earth.

Dee Evetts (1996-2001) is a carpenter in New York City by day, and by night the moderator of the Spring Street Haiku Group.

Maureen Gorman (1997-2001) believes her study of haiku is a perfect complement to her work as a professional counselor.

A. C. Missias (2001) is, besides editor of *Acorn* and owner of red fox press, a very considerable poet and bridge player.

Kohjin Sakamoto (1997-2001) is a university professor who has written haiku in English as well as Japanese for over two decades.

Alan Summers (2000-1) co-editor of *haijinx*, and founder of *haijin no hadaka* transmedia projects, lives writing haiku when he can!

George Swede (2000-1) lives and writes in Toronto and San Antonio Tlyacapan, Mexico.

RMA Editors-Emeritus: **Lee Gurga** (1998), **Yvonne Hardenbrook** (1996-8), **John Hudak** (1996-7), **H. F. Noyes** (1996-9), **Francine Porad** (1996), **Ebba Story** (1996), **Jeff Witkin** (1996-2000).

The RMA Process

DURING THE TWELVE MONTH PERIOD December 1, 2000 through November 30, 2001, over 2000 haiku and related works by over 1500 different authors have been nominated for inclusion in *the loose thread: The Red Moon Anthology 2001* by our staff of 11 editors from hundreds of sources from around the world. These sources are, in the main, the many haiku books and journals published in English, as well as the internet. Each editor is assigned a list of books and journals, but is free to nominate any work, from any source, s/he feels is of exceptional skill. In addition, the editor-in-chief is responsible for reading all of these sources, which ensures every possible source is examined by at least two nominating persons.

Editors may neither nominate nor vote for their own work.

Contest winners, runners-up and honorable mentions are automatically nominated.

When the nominating period concludes, all haiku and related works which receive nomination are placed (anonymously) on a roster. The roster is then sent to each of the judges, who votes for those works s/he considers worthy of inclusion. At least 5 votes (of the 10 judges, or 50%—the editor-in-chief does not have a vote at this stage) are necessary for inclusion in the volume. The work of editors must also receive at least 5 votes from the other 9 editors (55%) to merit inclusion.

The editor-in-chief then compiles these works, seeks permissions to reprint, and assembles them into the final anthology.